THE PEOPLE'S GUIDE TO COLLEGE APPLICATIONS

A WEEK-BY-WEEK APPROACH TO WRITING, CONNECTING, AND GETTING IN

JILL CONSTANTINO, PhD

Prometheus Books
Essex, Connecticut

 Prometheus Books

An imprint of The Globe Pequot Publishing Group, Inc.
64 South Main Street
Essex, CT 06426
www.globepequot.com

Copyright © 2026 by Jill Constantino

All rights reserved. No part of this book may be reproduced in any form or by any electronic or mechanical means, including information storage and retrieval systems, without written permission from the publisher, except by a reviewer who may quote passages in a review.

British Library Cataloguing in Publication Information available

Library of Congress Cataloging-in-Publication Data

Names: Constantino, Jill author
Title: The people's guide to college applications : a week-by-week approach to writing, connecting, and getting in / Jill Constantino.
Description: Essex, Connecticut : Prometheus, [2026] | Audience: Ages 18 | Audience: Grades 10–12 | Summary: "In this week-by-week guide, a former Harvard writing teacher and dean takes students and their families on a journey to explore their identities, write their stories, connect with one another, navigate the stress of college admissions, and find a fabulous future"—Provided by publisher.
Identifiers: LCCN 2025033044 (print) | LCCN 2025033045 (ebook) | ISBN 9781493091546 paperback | ISBN 9781493091553 epub
Subjects: LCSH: College applications—United States—Handbooks, manuals, etc. | Universities and colleges—Admission
Classification: LCC LB2351.52.U6 C67 2026 (print) | LCC LB2351.52.U6 (ebook)
LC record available at https://lccn.loc.gov/2025033044
LC ebook record available at https://lccn.loc.gov/2025033045

For my mom and my dad, who taught me wide-eyed wonder.

CONTENTS

Introduction xiii

WEEK 1, AUGUST 23–29: How to Use This Book 1
   Students 2
      Value Your Uncertainty 2
      Make Peace with Your Worries 3
      Give Yourself a Pep Talk 3
      Visit Some Places 4
      Talk to Your Parents 4
      Think about Money 4
      Be Open 5
   Concerned Adults 5

WEEK 2, AUGUST 30–SEPTEMBER 5: Who Loves You? 9
   Students 10
      Be Considerate 10
      Select Your Letter Writers 11
      Prepare a Resume for Your Letter Writers and for Yourself 12
      Gather Materials to Give to Your Letter Writers 15
      Write Your Letter Writers 15
      Visit Your Letter Writers 18
      Sign Up to Take the SAT or the ACT One More Time (Maybe) . 19
   Concerned Adults 20
      Consider the Stresses of Senior Year 20
      Suggest Letter Writers 23

Build Some Resumes. 23
Offer Help to Your Child as They Write Their Teacher Emails . . . 24
Ask If Your Student Has Met with Their Teachers
    and Counselor. 24
Celebrate Those Letter Requests. 26
Check in about Future SAT and ACT Tests 26

WEEK 3, SEPTEMBER 6–12: Wait, Who Am I?. 27

Students 28
Write Three Lists That You Save Forever 28
Share Your Lists with the People You Love 29
Acknowledge That You Will Be Stepping Away. 30
Consider Your Future 30
What Would You Do in the Movie Version of Your Life? 31
Combine Your Audacious Dream with the More Practical One . . 32
Visit College Websites 33

Concerned Adults 34
Write Three Lists. 34
Compare Your Lists with Your Student's Lists 34
Research Colleges and Their Qualities. 35
Make Your Life Better. 36
Do Some Fun Things 36
Suspend Money Worries. 39
Go to FAFSA and Read 40

WEEK 4, SEPTEMBER 13–19: Where Am I Going? 41

Students 43
Write a Truly Atrocious First Draft for Your Principal Essay 43
Pick Images, Stories, and Ideas from Your Lists for Your Draft . . . 44
Focus on Something Tiny, Then Expand into Your Bigger Ideas . . . 47
Be Humble and Self-Aware 48
Take on the Big, Little, Good, Bad, Ugly, and Beautiful. 50
Expect Major Overhauls as You Draft. 51
Let's Make a College List 51

CONTENTS

Concerned Adults 56
   Make Your Person Write Their Rough Draft 56
   Breathe. 56
   Write Your Own College List for Your Student. 57
   Make a Spreadsheet with Dates 59
   Drop Those Colleges onto a Map 62
   Picture Your Student and Yourself in All Those Places 63
   Tell Two People about Your Week 3 Life Betterment Plan 63

WEEK 5, SEPTEMBER 20–26: Am I Quirky Enough? 65
   Students. 67
      Lovingly Consider Your Rough Draft Material 67
      Begin Working with That Rough Draft Material 68
      Search for Your Thesis 74
      Write Your Thesis 75
      Identify Your Most Charming Characteristics. 78
      Chunk Up Your Essay 80
      Consider Ending with a Chunk about Your Future 81
   Concerned Adults 82
      Help Your Student with Their Essay. 82
      Don't Help Your Student with Their Essay 84
      Help Your Student Identify Their Most Salient Characteristics
         While You Identify Your Own 84
      Gather Your Resources. 85
      Check on Recommendation Letters 86
      Sketch a List of Your Student's Extracurriculars. 87
      Research Your Money Opportunities and Challenges 87

WEEK 6, SEPTEMBER 27–OCTOBER 3: Getting Things Just Right . . 91
   Students. 93
      Share Your Application Process 93
      Take Essay Feedback and Change Things (Or Don't) 94
      Be Resilient as You Draft, Rearrange, and Change Your Essay . . . 98
      Make Sure Your Structure Is Working. 99

    Fill in the Blanks. 100
    Prepare for Supplemental Essays and the Activities Section. 101
    Double-Check and Remind 102
Concerned Adults 103
    Be Supportive 103
    Help Your Child Get Sleep 103
    Sit with Your Person as They Complete Their Application 104
    Don't Sit with Your Person If It Feels Wrong 104
    Talk to Your Student about Extracurriculars. 105
    Get Yourself an Extracurricular 105
    Buy a Piece of Equipment and Practice Your Activity. 106

WEEK 7, OCTOBER 4–10: Loosening Up and Closing In 107
Students. 108
    Honor the Time of Your Extracurricular Hours 108
    Use Numbers to Quantify Your Magnificence 109
    Use Precise or Unexpected Verbs 110
    Consider Your Leadership Broadly 111
    Consider Short-Lived, Less Important, and Past Activities 112
    Group Activities to Save Space and Demonstrate Passion. 113
    Add One More Story to Your Essay, Then Distribute 115
Concerned Adults 115
    Help Your Person Cut Words 115
    Edit the Extracurriculars. 116
    Consider a Money Plan 117
    Have a Family Money Culture Conversation 118
    Make Peace with Your Economic Preparations and Situation 119
    Discuss Financial Responsibility and Its Implications 120
    Problem Solve 122

WEEK 8, OCTOBER 11–17: Fulfilling Your Wildest Dreams 125
Students. 126
    Cut Words in Your Principal Essay 126
    Consider Your Principal Essay: Is It Beautiful and Complete? . . .129

CONTENTS

    Write Your "How Will You Add to Our Community?" Essay. . . . 130
    Write Your "Why Our University?" Essay 132
    Continue to Paint Yourself Vibrantly True. 133
    Read Through Your Entire Application, One More Time 135
    Hit the "Celebrate" Button. 135
Concerned Adults 136
    Celebrate the First Application Submission 136
    As Your Person Peruses College Websites, You Should
        Do the Same 136
    Keep Editing; Keep Cutting Words 136
    Help Your Student Refine Their List 136
    Do Emotional and Logistical Triage. 137
    Look at Your Schedule and Consider Your Fate 137
    Hey, Maybe You Should Take a Trip This Summer?. 138

WINTER: Beyond Failure and Success **139**
Students 141
    Submit One Application Every Few Days. 141
    Or Take a Week or Two Off. 141
    Double-Check All Your Portals 141
    As You Keep Going or as You Rest, Consider Stress 142
    Interviews 143
    Don't Get into a School 146
    Get into a School! 146
    Read Everything, Log into the Portals, and Be a Joiner 147
Concerned Adults 148
    Stay Steady. 148
    If Your Kid Is Taking a Breather in November, Don't Worry 148
    Be Curious about Supplemental Essays 149
    Consider a Visit to a New Category of Colleges 149
    Understanding College Decisions: Acceptance! 149
    Deferral. 150
    Waitlist. 151

THE PEOPLE'S GUIDE TO COLLEGE APPLICATIONS

SPRING: Abundance **155**
    Students 156
        Consider the Spring Landscape 156
        Contemplate Your Acceptances 158
        Write Letters of Continued Interest for Waitlist Schools 159
        Visit Your Lead Possibilities 163
        Negotiate Financial Offers If Necessary 164
        Make a Decision Slowly and Surely 164
        Thank Everyone 165
    Concerned Adults 165
        Hold Space for the Little Pain 165
        Listen to the Bigger Pain 166
        Calibrate Your Response to Danger 167
        Hold Space for the Joy 168
        Visit and Revisit Colleges 169
        Model Good Decision-Making 170
        Shift a Little 173

SUMMER: The Cataclysm **175**
    Students 176
        Keep Simple Rules for Yourself 176
        No Regrets 176
        Be Relentlessly Curious 177
        Be Kind 177
        Spend Your Energy (Or Rest) 179
        Do Hard Things 180
        And One More Thing 181
    Concerned Adults 182
        Take Action on Irrational Worry 182
        Throw Your Whole Self into an Extra-Long Sheets Project 182
        Give Advice 183
        Mark All the Lasts 183

CONTENTS

Prepare a Scrapbook, Journal, or Picture Album 183
Make a Communication Contract 184
Hook Your Leg Out the Door and Slow the World by Dragging
    Your Foot against Time 184

Addendum Essay Examples 185
Acknowledgments 201

INTRODUCTION

THE SITUATION

Touring colleges with my oldest child, we were determined to chew up every bit of advice and digest every single morsel of information. The messages were clear and surprisingly consistent. Everything was going to be just fine as long as my daughter found "the right fit" and figured out how to convey her "authentically quirky self." But it's a big ask to be quirky on cue. And to be authentically quirky when you're not yet sure who you are is even trickier. To present the right quirk to your fit-school is near impossible, especially when you haven't yet figured out what these institutions do or what happens inside the sets of buildings or how all of the people on college tours seem to understand architecture in such a nuanced way that they have refined opinions on favorite eras for campus design. All of this makes for an insecure student.

Put a similarly insecure parent (by which I mean a person who worries and loves) beside that student, a parent who simultaneously believes that their child can do anything but insecurely doubts that their child will get in anywhere, a parent who is so scared about money and the ending of this most important stage of their life, a parent who is pretty sure that their whole caretaking endeavor has been inadequate because they are also feeling a bit confused about architecture styles, and a parent who then projects this anxiety onto their child, demanding that essays should have been completed months ago. Things get tough.

Time is getting short, and adults have this one last great parenting act to accomplish. But their child is either hardened against parental overreach or irritated by its tone. Concerned adults must launch their babies with the brilliance of philosopher-therapists and the patience of a bonsai sculptor. And they must do it all while pretending that they're just hanging out, chill.

The kid, on the other hand, is just now figuring out hard work, self-care, and responsibility. It's a bit daunting to also consider the rest of their life, to select from a whole world of possibilities, to fine tune their identity, to understand the geographic map of the United States and the cultural differences among those places in order to determine their perfect "fit." And they must learn how to be quirky? To represent themselves as quirky?! No wonder that despair plants itself around the middle of junior year and grows like a weed well into the next year.

Students reach September of senior year and begin a wide-eyed panic. Parents, who began their panic a few days earlier, release I-told-you-so exasperation. Collectively, they spiral into an overwhelming crisis, blaming school, work, social media, and their mothers. Grown-ups wonder if they have screwed it all up as their young people are either white-knuckled dependent or locked away in their rooms. Students find it hard to breathe, let alone construct a positive and resilient portrayal of self that feels right. The intense cultural pressure to do good, be well, and achieve phenomenal success often undercuts our very ability to do these things.

THE ESSENTIAL QUESTION

The application process can bring forth some hard questions: What do you want to do with your life? What *can* you do with your life? What makes you special? Does anything make you special? Are you smart enough? Are you good enough?

And for adult caregivers: Who is this creature you have created? Don't you think you could have prepared them better? Couldn't you

INTRODUCTION

have asked for a little more? Look at your anxious sweetie! Why did you ask so much of them? Can't you see that it was too much?

It's okay. Put these questions away. There is only one question that matters: Who are you? It's such a sweet question, really. In this life of running around and trying to be someone, we tend to forget that we have always been someone, that our someone is actually quite lovely, and that this someone is capable of shapeshifting into so many gorgeous forms. We forget the beautiful stories that consume our hours—the time we helped our baby brother put socks on his tiny feet, how we like to sit on the orange chair by a window with spider webs, how we can make Bolognese sauce and skateboard ramps. We cease to hold as important our cool style or Cool Ranch Doritos. We forget that we love the color green, films about whales, and relief maps. We devalue our algorithmic ways, our babysitting, our grit. We gloss over our sacred stories of the homes, fields, and grocery stores that have helped shape our vulnerable little selves and bodies. But with complete certainty, I guarantee that you are already quite remarkable.

Oh, and the forms that we may become! Something about filling out an application funnels our brains into a handful of possibilities—an engineer, a doctor, a lawyer, a teacher. But there are so many subdivisions of those categories and so many millions of critical jobs we have yet to even invent. We could be plastic ethicists, book binders, piano detailers, artisanal plumbers, death doulas, AI sensitivity consultants, catastrophe ameliorators, insect collectors, history fixers. Oh, so many things! There are so many ways to present our current selves and our future projections of self to our families, to schools, to the world. It's a phenomenal process.

The answer to who we are is a past, present, and future endeavor with the potential to connect us to people we love, see ourselves in new ways, inspire change, make loved ones proud, open doors, and create meaning for this life. All we have is this one little life, and without our brains considering it, this life can get a bit stuck, waiting for others to define it. Applying to college hits at exactly the right moment, when high school runs out and our cultures so often call for next steps. Young people work through the tiny, big, beautiful, sad, and important things and events that make them who they are. They compile vignettes toward a better understanding of their past and their identity as they launch themselves into a newly considered future.

Meanwhile, concerned adults figure out how they relate to this skittish, stressed out, silent, insecure, overconfident, angry, oblivious, eager creature who lives in their house. The college application offers an opportunity for parents to lovingly package up a childhood gone so fast while reassessing who they are as people, also moving quite rapidly through time. With diminishing caretaking, an uptick in elder-care, shifting brain space, creakier bodies, and tuition-related economic stress, parents might need to reassess some of their own ways of being and fortify their structures of contentment. This time period offers them an opportunity to gather up their own identities, brush them off, and walk square-shouldered into the beauty ahead.

ANSWERING THAT ESSENTIAL QUESTION

So, who are you? Now we know the essential question, but how do we answer it? We write. Writing is thinking. *The People's Guide to College Applications* provides a step-by-step process with small goals and many illustrative examples to launch you into writing your life and your identity. This book encourages very bad first drafts and aggressive rewrites. Students will learn how to center themselves as they locate their most fabulous characteristics. They will write a lot, putting so many thoughts into the world that some of those sentences will have no option but to be great. And then they will cut for concision, removing words and ideas that get in the way of meaning and understanding.

INTRODUCTION

Students will learn to cut repetitive language and general statements ("the world has a balance of good and bad," for example) to make room for experiences and sensory details that tell the same story ("the yellow food truck served spicy tacos on a bitter January after my friend's car accident"). They will figure out how to question their premises humbly. (*Wait, maybe the world isn't so balanced for all people? Maybe I have some privilege that helps it feel that way? Or maybe some life situations require more resilience? Is my grief the same as others?*) Students will practice speculating on future possibilities even though they are certainly unsure, and then they will write about those speculations in bold, true, and hopeful ways. ("I want to be a therapist to show people how an even balance can potentially exist between good and bad." *No, maybe something bigger and truer?* "I want to be a lawyer who advocates for people in dire situations so that I create a more balanced world.")

In the meantime, parents will become good accountability partners. They will find new ways to empathize with their students' processes of self-definition. Concerned adults will break through the fortresses of insecurity that keep their children distant. By understanding the timeline of college applications and the student needs that arise along the path, parents will find it easier to access the helpful energy, hopeful patience, and vulnerability that create connection. And parents will have an opportunity to consider their own futures as they write in new ways, if they want, if they have time, if they are so inclined. Writing is an amazing tool for life betterment.

This book will remove roadblocks from the college application by systematically stepping through each stage of the application process. Students often sit frozen, waiting for brilliance. They are accustomed to writing with immediate deadlines so they aren't sure what to do with a month or more. They are experts at five-paragraph night-before-a-due-date desperation, but many of them have little experience exploring themselves through writing or even using the word *I* in essays. They seem to be waiting for someone to give them permission to be themselves, to break out of the structures they have learned. Though they are experts at reporting on texts and analyzing facts and quotes, they often don't feel comfortable speculating, exploring, or wondering in their writing. Students will learn to write openly, without paralyzing expectation, toward new understandings.

These processes of exploration may be even more uncomfortable for parents. We want our babies to know it all already—to have figured out the exact path that will bring them comfort and joy. We may even feel like we have failed our children if they do not yet have a developed sense of self and direction. (No, we have not failed them. The world is complicated, and they are so young.) And being that college can be pricey, we don't want to waste our money on uncertainty because, of course, money is finite and uncertainty is infinite. And further, many adults come from eras and cultures in which people plan and study for a particular vocation, whereas the current job market is considerably more fluid. Considering the uncertainties in our children and the process, it's easy for concerned adults to back away and throw up their hands. This book offers weekly projects, support ideas, and you-don't-need-to-worry-about-this-yet markers to calm the overwhelmed.

Even if young people feel free to dream their way into some wild and wonderful future, they lack the experience and self-confidence to project a hazy potential dream (*I would love to meet a mermaid*) into a confident aspirational sentence (*as an anthropologist, I will study northern European sea-faring communities and their processes of myth formation*). They don't know how to take a broad, not-sure-what-else-to-do choice (*I'll go into business*), into a hand-tailored unique creation of problem-solving joy ("What business? To solve what problem?" *Well, in my life, my grandpa is a bit of a disaster behind the wheel. I love to drive! Maybe I could make a business that pairs newly licensed teenagers up with those who can no*

INTRODUCTION

longer drive! [My mom thinks this is a very bad idea.] I use Uber Teen once in a while. What about my own brand of an Uber Elder?) We will learn how to persist in ideas through layered questions and drafts.

This book encourages audaciousness through research. As families pore over college websites, they will come to understand the amazing opportunities available. Students will dive into faculty bios to learn the world of opportunity open to them. Then, they will communicate with their new idols of intellect. They will practice asking good questions as they become motivated to learn their ways into the future.

As the process approaches due dates, families are encouraged to visit more campuses and stay in the shifting ground of college decision and identity formation. This time period, so squished and uncertain, can actually be great fun. While official tours are helpful, it's a blast to throw frisbees on quads sprinkled with adorable young people, to check for open doors on beautiful buildings, and to sit on couches under chandeliers in libraries. How does a decadent coffee drink from a campus coffee shop taste when it is consumed amid studying students and their stickered laptops? As our kids see how happy and interesting and fun these spaces are, their enthusiasm builds and they naturally brush parents off a bit, engaging more enthusiastically and independently in their application processes. Students will learn to adore every college they consider in order to lessen the stress of economic variables, rejections, and dream schools.

Parents may find comfort in this book's permission to hold on to their babies for just a little bit longer. It's okay for adults to assert opinions and express worries. It's okay to nag, cajole, and even discipline students into finding their best futures. Students will figure out how to step into independence without losing their vulnerability and thoughtfulness. They must seek editorial support yet must also trust their intuitions to reject editorial suggestions. They must dream their futures aggressively and passionately against the insecurity that they feel and against the concerns that their parents may feel. Parents and kids must hold tight while letting go.

As family structures shift, parents and students must reconfigure connection. Once a child hits college, they need to make their own way. This book helps parents embrace FaceTime and Snapchat so they may persistently check in on those students who are making their own way. Their children will surely need to know how the dog is doing! They will be curious about the new kitchen flooring. They will definitely want information on laundry machines.

Students, you can call your adult when you're a couple of minutes from class. They'll know you're going to class! They will project their worry on to you for just a short bit. They will tell you they love you. Text them that you're in the library or at the gym, when maybe you've only made it there mentally . . . but you're on your way, really. Call when you're sad. Have fun when you're having fun. Ask for cookies. You're going to kill it!

Week 1, August 23–29

HOW TO USE THIS BOOK

The People's Guide to College Applications provides weekly to-do lists for the college applicant and their support team. The program begins at the entrance to senior year because that's when many students really get going. If you are reading these words in the summer before senior year, during junior year, or even before that, you can step through just as effectively and at a comfortable pace, maybe. Some people feel better luxuriating in the time and details. Others need to fly. Know yourself, your way, and your unique structural circumstance, and be okay with it all.

This time period can be tricky for families because everyone may be a little freaked out about the huge changes on the way. Parents doubt their own parenting, and students live in horror that they will disappoint everyone. People fight. This is normal, and kind of sweet. You care about each other. Throughout this book, I will suggest many ways to connect. Try some! It's okay if you fight your way through, and it's okay if it all feels kind of disastrous. As your person prepares to leave you (either by entering a new phase of life or moving to a new town), you all have to shift some structures, separate a little to create independence, and hold on for dear life. This is confusing. This is senior year. This is love.

If you're a student, you might be feeling bad that you haven't done more already. If you're a concerned adult, you might be upset with your kid because they haven't done more. You might be upset with yourself that you haven't figured out a good way to compel your kid to do more. You might be looking around, thinking that everyone else is better prepared. But the truth is, all of you are in the middle of it already, and none of you are almost done.

Applying to college is just one important step in this lifelong process of figuring yourself out. You've actually been working on your own personal narrative for your whole life. But it's super tough to find the confidence to write it all down, pretty it up, and throw it into the world. It's near impossible to do this with any dignity while your concerned adults are anxiously fretting. Doing it while you're also trying to do the intellectual, emotional, and physical work of high school? That's a lot. The process is overwhelming. It's not just you. It's overwhelming for everyone. But it's also pretty cool.

Even after this business of applying to college is over, you will need to keep seeking yourself, uncovering your idiosyncratic contributions to the world. There are no definitive answers, just a forever process. And because it is forever, you don't really have to get it exactly right at this minute. If you do, the game is over. You just have to start playing. It won't be perfect, but it almost definitely will be beautiful. Because you are beautiful; I promise.

STUDENTS

Value Your Uncertainty

Who are you? Throughout this book, I will ask this question in many different forms, and you will answer it in a billion ways. Your job is not to find the perfect answer but to find as many answers as you can, as fast as you can, without really thinking that much at first. You are what? Sixteen? Seventeen? Eighteen? You are so young. You can't possibly have perfect answers for such open-question ridiculousness! So just throw a bunch of possible answers out. This is the process! You must learn to be good at throwing unsure ideas into the world. No brilliant process has ever begun with certainty.

If we were already certain about it, then we wouldn't need any brilliance, would we? Brilliance always starts in an unsure, not-knowing place. Value your uncertainty!

Make Peace with Your Worries

Are you worried that you're too late, too immature, too lazy? What will happen? Will you disappoint your parents, give your parents exactly what they want, deny yourself what you want, pick wrong, pick right and then not get in, not be able to afford it, not succeed? What if I told you that every single person who ever applied to college worried in exactly this way? No kidding, every single one. Well, I've met a few people who say they aren't worried or stressed. Maybe they're not. Maybe they know what they're doing. I am so happy for them! But I don't completely believe them.

Give Yourself a Pep Talk

Self-doubt is not productive. There's not much to be done with "I can't do it." Yet "I can't do it" can feel entirely true because the tasks of a college application are so daunting and so involved. We double down on our "I can't do it" and announce it to the world, thereby creating a little team of doubters—people who tell us, "yes, you can," but who certainly harbor some doubt, we know, because we put it there. This means that we have to do extra great to show those people who doubt us, which can make us feel paralyzed. It's a tricky cycle.

But often, there's a tiny part of us—sometimes the tiniest, tiniest part—that knows we can certainly do this thing well. We just have to go with that part. We have to. We really don't have a choice if we hope to avoid the boring cycle of nothing-outcomes. Make a deal with yourself right now: "I will not self-deprecate to anyone, even to myself."

Ironically, it takes a great deal of humility to be confident, to refrain from burdening others with our self-doubt. In gathering our confidence, we must recognize that people actually aren't that dependent on our successes or failures, that they all exist in their own spaces, in their own stories, and in their own worries. The humblest thing in the world, actually, is to gather up your confidence and try really hard. Try hard! Be you. You can do it!

Visit Some Places

Ideally, you'll step onto a few campus lawns and into a few institutional buildings to smell the dirt and the floor cleaner, but more on that later. For now, just pause in the places where you are. What do you love about the little tree on the corner? Do you like the feel of that tree next to your shoulder? Would you like to live in a place with lots of trees? How do you feel when you are surrounded by tons of people—at a pep rally, on a parade route, at a festival, or during rush hour? Do you feel part of things, scared, anxious, lonely, alive, happy? Are you cold? Do you mind? Is it cozy? Do you love water? Does it beckon you, away from important things?

Do you feel like an outsider in your hometown? In your school? Are there people like you there? Do you feel like you belong? The beautiful thing about next steps is that you'll get a chance to experience what it feels like in other places. Maybe you'll find a sense of belonging like you've never had! Figure out what makes you feel good.

Talk to Your Parents

Pretend you are their parent. Listen to them in your best parental way. They are so cute, so neurotic, so worried. It's okay to patronize them a little bit. Tell them that everything will be okay and that there are many wonderful schools out there. It will work out. Tell them that this is a journey and you'll be with them the whole way.

Think about Money

Money is not so powerful, little pieces of paper and metal. It sure acts powerfully, though. It has the ability to stress, prohibit, differentiate, and demean. It knows how to situate itself between you and the people and places you love. You have to pay attention to it, but don't let it shut down your possibilities yet. There are still many financial unknowns. Right now, all you must know is that college can be economically stressful. Hold that reality gently in your hands, like a tiny puppy with sharp teeth.

It's not the right time to flee from danger and cross "apply to college" off your to-do list. You don't yet know how much your potential colleges will cost. Critically, the sticker price of a school is rarely the price you pay. Many of the most expensive schools are actually free for people who live below a particular income level. Many seemingly expensive schools can be relatively cheap for those in the middle class. There is a financial puzzle to be solved, and excellent applications are key. Hold on to your puppy!

Be Open
You might change your mind on so many things: what you want to do, who you want to be, and who you are. We are these mutable little creatures who encounter so many logistical, social, emotional, and ideological turning points. We can flip upside down and back again in a minute. Doors close and open throughout our lives, and we get to walk through, walk back, and walk through again. Stay open to the opportunities, be resilient with the twists and turns, and trust your intuition.

CONCERNED ADULTS
Look, I'm not going to boldly subject-head your steps this first week because I want to have a straightforward little talk with you. Throughout this book, I suggest many wonderful things that you can do for your student and that you can do for yourself. I give you weekly lists of instructions, which include helpful advice and sample talks for your kid. I suggest opportunities for introspective questions, gentle reminders, and forceful directives, which include

flowery pep talks and aggressive manipulations. I offer self-help activities for you. On top of all this, I give your student so many big, little, simple, and complicated steps for forward movement. Your young person may ignore these and need you to push them forward. They may want you to read the steps and then feed them with the process.

But listen. You don't have to do any of these things. At this point in life, you have your way. You probably have many ways that have proven reliable. I honor this with my whole heart. I hope that you will grab what you need to stay afloat and ignore any directives or advice that threaten to push you further underwater. I imagine you trying to work, clean, bathe, fix, mow, solve, forgive, remove, purchase. Are you trying to get a child to eat and another to stop eating? Is it already way past everyone's bedtime? Is your boss mad at you? Are you running the place and no one knows it? Does your partner have zero ability to find the sesame oil? Is your child totally functioning while also completely falling apart?

Your hands are full, my lovely. Don't worry if you don't get to your section. Ask for help if you want someone else to manage it. If you can't ask for help, just be proud that you're doing your best, even if your best sucks on some days. Please, take it easy on yourself.

It's an odd thing to grow a little creature from fierce love and protectiveness through days and years which include so many versions of mastery and collapse. We watch our child dismantle a good toy and simultaneously know that they will become (a) an engineer or (b) a felon. The roller coaster of struggle, discovery, pain, and joy moves so fast, there's little time to understand and become comfortable with the ride. By the time our young people reach their late teenage years, regardless of whether they have siblings, even if they've been really great kids, we're starting to feel creaky and exhausted. Our neural pathways of worry are so deeply etched, there's almost no escaping anxiety. We've been so patient for so long. And we're really not sure they're going to make it. The child still sobs wildly over history papers. Or forgets they have history papers. They seem incapable of responding to wake-up alarms or fire alarms or relationship alarms, like really incapable. We find vape pens, beer bottles, irresponsibility, and sadness all over the place even though they know how ridiculously paranoid we've become about these precise things. But still we envision their flourishing and hold hope that they will go to college—because it seems like a decent next step. And it is!

I'm all for trade schools, artistic thrivings, ambitious tech start-ups, and other launch pads that nurture talent and growth as they redesign the high school–college trajectory, but if your family is education curious, college is quite a wonderful step. Your child may find a niche that fits them well. They might encounter a friend group that is worldly, nice, smart, and politically aligned with your ideals. They may be drawn to a subject matter and a study abroad program that will take them (and you, when you visit) to new cultures and countries. They may become passionate about a topic that solves global problems. They will make you proud, they will mess up, they will grow, they will mature in a somewhat safe environment with responsible adults around. It's a pretty good opportunity.

Parents tend to fall on a continuum as they approach this phase and the college application. Some have a million ideas on exactly how their child should fill out application questions and exactly what their child should write in their college essays. They jot notes to themselves about businesses their person might start to demonstrate initiative. They research Himalayan peaks that might be trekked to get a leg up on the competition. Ridiculously ready for the magnum opus of their parenting life, they will do anything to reach the height and protect their child from suffering. This book helps them to step back so that they can trust their child and the process.

On the other end of the spectrum, there are many people who believe that kids must really figure things out for themselves. If they are going to make it through college on their own, they must make it into college on their own. Sink or swim. This approach comes in useful if you can't get your person to talk with you.

But the reality is this: it's very difficult to work through the complex economic, academic, and social aspects of the college application process alone. Navigating FAFSA (Free Application for Federal Student Aid), Naviance, and the applications in all their forms (e.g., Common, Universal, Common Black, Coalition, system-shared, and individual school) can be bewildering. Picking colleges and an initial path is a massive logistical, intellectual, and emotional task. Students and parents need support networks.

Moreover, writing is something best done in conversation with other people. All the books on the market are edited. All the writing that people do should be edited. A second or third or fourth set of eyes is crucial for any high-level work and for becoming better at any task. It is not cheating to consider your life with other people and then to have them help you formulate it with structural criticisms, grammar corrections, and word cuts. Your young person needs you as they apply to college.

They have run, crawled, and fought their way through twenty-five-and-a-half miles of the growing-up marathon, and now they might be a bit crampy and locked up. This idea that they are leaving you and that they need to make it on their own and that they might disappoint you can be a lot to handle. You don't need to do any one particular thing to be there for them. You just have to be there.

And one important note: There are many inequities in the systems and processes that structure our world. Money, education, history, and luck impact people variably. Some students will find an easier path to support than others. Some adults will find an easier path in their caretaking. Inevitably, there will be many students and adults who walk through a bit lost and without support. Once you help your baby, help others. We can do this.

Week 2, August 30–September 5

WHO LOVES YOU?

This week, you hit the ground running, leap into action, set things in motion, dive in! You just have to close your eyes and go. On the other side of *go*, things are so much calmer. But that first step is a doozy.

When my husband and I bought our farm, we knew it was a bit ridiculous. We are people of shockingly few practical skills. To run a farm, take care of a centuries-old farmhouse, and have a fourth kid without a good stash of cash is simply not feasible. But it sounded interesting and fun. So I just started telling people we were doing it. I started showing them plans for potential flower fields and pond revitalization projects. I told the children we would get a dog. They started drawing adorable pictures of bucolic scenes—red barns and apples trees. I told my boss. Once the community was on board, either with grave concerns or cheerleader-y ideas, it was done.

You must declare your intentions to your community now—your teachers, your counselor, your parents, your friends. If you are an adult who thinks college might be the right direction for your kid, look them in the eye and tell them that you know they can do it. Even if you aren't sure, there's part of you that knows. Stand on that part and declare it. If you are a student, tell your friends that you're thinking about UCLA. (Maybe you thought about it once. Think about it again now. There. You're thinking about UCLA.)

Your community will rally behind you, with you, ready to propel you in whatever way they tend to propel you.

STUDENTS

Be Considerate

You literally can't apply to college on your own. You must start this whole process with your teachers and your school counselor because you have a favor to ask them and they need time to complete this favor. Taking care of them takes care of you.

In fact, taking care of the people around you is the number one thing you have to do to get into schools. Doing well on your applications, in college, and in life involves being nice to people. Colleges want to admit nice students, considerate people, and kids who play well with others. They're trying to build community, and that process happens most efficiently when people aren't too explicitly selfish. So be totally considerate of everyone in your life from now on, okay?

You probably are, explicitly. But there might be little ways in which stresses pervade your subconscious and seep out of you into the lives of others. Take care of yourself to minimize your stress and prepare yourself for openness. Ironically, in the midst of all the logistical, developmental, and emotional upheavals of now—right when you are diving deep within yourself to enter this extraordinarily personal project—it is the perfect time to consider others and involve them in your life and your projects. As you move through each step of this application process, pause and wonder about all the people who connect to you. How does your life impact their lives? Let's start with your teachers.

Your teachers and your school counselor need to prepare recommendation letters for you ASAP, but they are busy people! They must write something long and great about you. And not just for you. Other students are probably asking them for letters, too. And your teachers have to prepare your lessons, teach you and your classmates all day, take care of their families, and walk their dogs. They need time. Ask now! I'll walk you through it.

Select Your Letter Writers

You must include two teacher letters in your applications to most schools. If you are great at math, include a high school math teacher. If you are amazing at science, pick your favorite science teacher. English teachers are always great because they can write! If your English teacher seems to know and appreciate you, pick them. Did you struggle in a class and then turn it around? That teacher might be able to write about your resilience. A teacher who is also the leader of one of your clubs or sports might have a lot to say because they know you in multiple contexts. Do you have a teacher who you love because they are so laid back? Do they calm you because they let things slide? This might be great, but it might not. Can you picture them putting time into a letter for you? If you can picture this, ask them! If you think they might let the task slide, don't ask them. Don't worry about finding someone famous. Just find the person who can and will share stories about you. (If you're not sure that this person exists, don't worry. I've got advice for you in the "Guidelines for Writing Academic and Professional Emails" textbox later in the chapter.)

Your school counselor also must write a recommendation letter for your application. (If you are homeschooled, your principal caretaker is considered your school counselor.) The counselor letter helps your college understand the context in which you were educated, how your GPA system works, how your particular course of study fits in with the offerings of your school, and how you have contributed to that school. Get in touch with them this week.

Prepare a Resume for Your Letter Writers and for Yourself

A resume is a lovely document that contains the curated you—a little piece of artfully constructed self that you hand to others. It is helpful when asking for application letters. It is often essential when seeking scholarships, awards, internships, and work. Some colleges will ask if you want to submit one along with your application.

If you already have a resume, that's great! Update it. Add your current extracurriculars and your burgeoning skills.

If you don't have a resume yet, let's build one. This baby will grow, change, and become more beautiful throughout your college application process as you remember the things you've done and as you recognize your skills. Throughout your life, you will come back to this resume to add, subtract, shift, and redesign. I've removed all of my cook and waitress jobs because my work doesn't involve those skills anymore, but I will never remove my bike messenger job. I like it on my resume because it shows people that I was once fierce-girl-strong-cool. Hopeful that I still am, I leave it on. You get to choose how to curate yourself. A resume is powerful.

Here is the most basic of templates. Make your headers bold, italic, or capitalized to differentiate. Add indentations. Center things. Use bullets. Use boxes and lines to make it pretty. Stylize to your heart's content, but no need for perfume or fancy fonts. You can choose full sentences or fragments when you create descriptions, but keep them consistent. For example, you might start each description with a verb in the past tense for things that happened in the past and a verb in the present tense for things that you are still doing. Resumes are loveliest when they are simple, elegant, and consistent. Search the internet for "resume templates" to give you more ideas.

A Simple Resume Template
NAME
Address I Phone Number I Email

Education
High School Name, City, State
Expected Graduation: month, year
GPA: unweighted and weighted
Course highlights: AP, IB, honors, specialized
Standardized tests: SAT, ACT, PSAT

Awards & Honors
Award, Scholarship, or Honor Society, year, description

Award, Scholarship, or Honor Society, year, description

Etc.

Extracurricular Activities
Organization or Team, role or position, date started to date ended or "present"
Description (include leadership roles and accomplishments in your descriptions)

Organization or Team, role or position, date started to date ended or "present"
Description (include leadership roles and accomplishments in your descriptions)

Etc.

Volunteer Experience
Organization, role or position, date started to date ended or "present"
Description (include the things you did and why they mattered)

Organization, role or position, date started to date ended or "present"
Description (include the things you did and why they mattered)

Etc.

Work Experience
Company Name, job title, date started to date ended or "present"
Description (include your responsibilities and what you learned)

Company Name, job title, date started to date ended or "present"
Description (include your responsibilities and what you learned)

Etc.

Skills
Technical: You might include PowerPoint, Python, or 3D printing.

Languages: You might say that you are fluent in French or that you know basic sign language.

Personal: This might include particular caretaking skills, public speaking, political organizing, or social media expertise.

Hobbies & Interests
You might include creative writing, skateboarding, or game playing, for example.

Just go for it, using great verbs to describe your accomplishments and skills.

Led, organized, coordinated, managed, facilitated, presented, communicated, collaborated, explained, persuaded, advocated, supported, participated, guided, encouraged, created, designed, developed, illustrated, solved, improved, streamlined, researched, analyzed, investigated, studied, compiled, programmed, debugged, tested, built, configured, installed, budgeted, fundraised, allocated, balanced, secured, mentored, coached, instructed, advised, educated, demonstrated, served, hosted, welcomed, assisted, prepared, cooked, cleaned, entertained, nurtured, fed, bathed, changed, read to, mowed, raked, trimmed, weeded, planted, watered, fertilized, mulched, landscaped, shoveled, swept.

Now, let's say you haven't illustrated, compiled, fertilized, or verbed that much in a professional or academic capacity. That's okay; I promise. If you haven't participated in any extracurriculars or if you haven't held any jobs, just cut those sections. Add a more general section titled "Skills" or "Experience," then list four or five of your top skills or experiences. Are you particularly good with numbers or words? Do you doodle like Picasso? Can you put together wonderful outfits or exciting adventures? Do you problem-solve for your siblings? Are you generous about changing the kitty litter or the car oil? Are you observant when someone changes their earrings or their state of mind? If you're still stuck, look at the verb list and figure out in which ways you have done any of those things. Start with what you do and add it to your resume. Honor your youth, your beginnings, and your perfectly great place in life.

Gather Materials to Give to Your Letter Writers

Now you have a resume! It might feel short, sweet, insecure, exhaustive, or exhausting, but you did it. You have a foundation to work with as you move toward "just right." Did you do a brag sheet for your school? Some schools assign and require these personal surveys as a way to help you get your application going. If you have a brag sheet started, read it over. Add to it. Think of a couple stories that might be the perfect examples for the particular questions. Fix your grammar. Finish questions you left unfinished. Don't worry if you don't have a brag sheet filled with stories! You have a resume!

Additionally, you might have an amazing essay you wrote, a portrait you sketched, a website you created, a social media account that shines. Gather one or two artifacts of your brilliance (your resume, your brag sheet, your essay, or portrait) and put them on your computer desktop, ready to send to your recommenders. Print them out, too. Some teachers prefer hard copies; printed materials might feel more formal, more polite, easier to find, easier to read. Some people like email; their computers act like little storage boxes for their stuff, and they appreciate the environmental benefits. You can print and email or do one or the other. Use your best judgment.

Write Your Letter Writers

You must craft a beautiful email and/or letter for each of your recommenders. First, make sure you spell their names correctly. Always be ridiculously careful with other people's names because they matter. Your school website will probably have a list.

Titles are really important, too: *Mr., Ms., Mx., Mrs., Miss, Dr., Professor.* These titles say and mean more than you might think. People with MDs are medical doctors and should be referred to as "Dr. [last name]." People with PhDs are doctors of philosophy, and you should also address them as "Dr. [last name]." You can call PhDs "Professor [last name]," if they are professors. But not all doctors are professors, so stick with *Dr.* if you're not sure.

Unmarried women might like to be addressed as *Miss* and married women might prefer *Mrs.*, but many women find these forms of address irritating: Why should their marriage status be of any interest to anyone? Many women prefer *Ms.* if they are not doctors. *Ms.* offers a parallel to *Mr.* in that neither title identifies marital status. But both of these titles are gendered. *Mx.* might be used for someone who identifies as nonbinary. Questions can be a lovely way to learn. You can ask a teacher in class tomorrow: "How would you like me to address you in an email?"

If you can't find information on your recommenders' title preferences after a little research, that's okay. Do your best. You don't have to be perfect, but doing your best to be respectful is kind and empathetic. You might be thinking to yourself, *I don't care what people call me,* but that doesn't mean that the person you are writing doesn't care. They might care for reasons that you don't or can't fully understand. Thinking about how people like to be addressed tells them that you honor who they are and how they think about themselves.

Follow these guidelines when you write your emails, now and forever:

Guidelines for Writing Emails to Your Recommenders

1. Err on the side of formality: Write "Dear Dr. Constantino," even if you call the person *Jill* or *bruh* in class.
2. Include a nice greeting: "I hope you are having a great week." Or "I loved the lesson on the quadratic formula." Or "The world feels a little dark lately, I hope you're holding up well." Or "I hope you had time to be out in the beautiful sunshine this week!" Try to sincerely connect with them (and everyone). It feels nice.

3. Get to the point pretty quickly: "I wondered if you would be willing to write me a letter of recommendation."
4. Tell them why you picked them and be specific: "I love the way you teach our class." "You seem to have an authentic love for the material, and I feel myself beginning to love it alongside of you." "It surprised me when you explained . . ." "When you told that story about your relationship to mathematical proofs, I realized . . ." "When you empathized with my struggle, I felt . . ." "I think you, more than anyone, know how I . . ."
5. Remind them why you are great. You might feel braggy or rude, telling people about the good things you have done, but it's an important skill to be gracefully confident. "It meant so much to me when you complimented my essay on Jane Eyre. I wasn't sure if I had it right or not, and now I have this newfound confidence . . ." Or "I thought you might be able to write about the presentation I did on naked mole-rats. You said it was one of the best in the class. I attached it here—because who doesn't want more naked mole-rats in their life!"
6. Be yourself. Your teacher probably has a good sense of who you are, even if you don't often directly interact. Being yourself in an email will assure them that they are right in their assessment. Your tone will also remind them to write about your personality. If you're funny, be funny. If you're really sweet, be really sweet. If you are particularly quiet in class and you worry that your teacher might not know you that well, don't worry. Guidelines 4 and 5 will help them know you better, so spend extra time and space on that part of your email.
7. Let your teachers know that you understand that you are asking them to do work for you. Show your gratitude in advance: "I recognize that we are in a busy time of the year. Thank you so much for considering my request."
8. Tell your teacher the timeline and submission instructions. "I hope to start wrapping up my application in the beginning of October [even if this is your very rosiest

projection for yourself], so if you can finish the letter and submit it through Naviance with the help of Ms. Poole [your school-assigned guidance counselor or your particular application portal] by September 21, I'd be so grateful."
9. Tell your teacher that you are attaching your resume or your brag sheet or a poem. Tell them why you think it might be helpful. "I am attaching my resume below. It will give you a summary of what I've been up to over the last few years. I hope the material is helpful as you write my letter. Please let me know if you have any questions." Or "I'm attaching a poem I wrote for your class. I thought that it might help you remember the quality of my work. Thank you for teaching that poem into me!"
10. Sign your name. Are you a *Sincerely* person? A *Best wishes* girl? A *You're the best!* guy? A *Have a nice day!* person? It's time to consider your professional persona.
11. Attach the material you gathered that provides the evidence of your brilliance! Remember to attach. I always forget to attach.

Visit Your Letter Writers

After you write your teachers and counselor, swing by their desks or offices to drop off a hard copy or just to check in. I know this can be terrifying if you're a quiet, hang-at-the-back-of-the-class, shy person, but try it out. It's good practice. And it will mean something to your teachers. Say something like this: "Hi, I wrote you an email to ask if you could write me a letter of recommendation for my college applications. Thanks so much for thinking about me." Recite it in your head before so you feel comfortable. You can do it! You have to, really. Life requires communication. And you're adorable. People want to communicate with you.

Your visit to your counselor is particularly important. You have to figure out how their letter will work. How do they gather information to write about you? How might you help them gather that information? How will they submit it and into what portal? How do they want your other teachers to submit their letters? What are the tricky things about the portal, and how can you ensure that your information gets to the right place, through the right technology, and at the right time? It's good to spend some time with that counselor, even if you already know the answers to all these questions. Counselors can be helpful! And, moreover, they need to know you to be maximally helpful as they write your letter. Visit them this week!

Sign Up to Take the SAT or the ACT One More Time (Maybe)

If you sign up right now, you still have time to take a test and submit your scores for the early deadlines. Even if your test scores don't arrive in time, most schools allow you to send them after you submit your application. So, let's think about whether you want to take those tests for the first time or for the second, third, or fourth times. Have you been avoiding them altogether? Or did you take one or both of them? Did you do okay? Are you curious to see how well you could do with a little more work, if you took a different test, if you did it on a different weekend? Was the test fun? Was it terrifying?

For those of you who have not taken the SAT or ACT yet: If you have the resources to pay the fee, or if you have the time to ask for a fee waiver, just do it. It might make a difference. It's good practice to take tests. It's good practice to study for tests. Your scores might make the difference between getting in and not getting in. They might make the difference between getting merit money and not getting merit money. You won't be able to doubt your decision if you do it. No regrets.

For those who have taken at least one test already: People will tell you that it's not necessary to take a test again if you're satisfied with your score. But they might not know what you are trying to achieve, and they certainly don't know the idiosyncratic ways of every university out there. If you are aiming for a top school (the top 20, 50, or even 100), the difference between a 1350 and a 1400 might matter. The difference between a 1550 and a 1590 might matter. You just don't know. Those spheres are wildly competitive. Just do it if you can swing it. No regrets.

People might tell you to pick the ACT or SAT based on your skill sets. But you can't really know which exam will feel more comfortable until you try them both. So consider taking the test you haven't taken yet. No regrets.

People might remind you that so many schools are now test optional that you can just decide not to submit. They might tell you that the testing system is a mess, because test-optional policies have skewed test scores upward. Yes, but every school uses test scores differently and evaluates particular test takers in the context of their life story. It's really hard to game the system in any clear way. So consider taking the test again. No regrets.

Studying really helps. Use Khan Academy to study. They partnered with the College Board to offer *free* online test prep for the SAT. The program is tailored to your particular results on past tests. It's great! The ACT offers a *free* study test. You can also find test prep books at the library.

And look, if you have a fair amount of test anxiety and you've given it your best shot and you are done, congratulations! Don't think about it again. No regrets.

CONCERNED ADULTS
Consider the Stresses of Senior Year

You are currently managing a lovely creature who believes they are grown and entirely independent, while displaying some alarming signs that they are not at all grown or independent. When my high school senior hit the side of the Taco Bell with our minivan, tried to cover the scratches with toothpaste, and then, when confronted, pretended not to notice the bashed-in door, I was concerned. He was concerned. My husband and I were angry about the lack of transparency. My son understood our anger but was frustrated when we were hesitant to let him do anything at all after that. He hadn't been drinking or messing around. He simply didn't remember to turn the steering wheel back after having cranked it to get close enough to the window—a simple mistake with a TikTok-inspired attempt to cover scratches. This was an important experience for him in his journey to become a good driver and a brave communicator. This was an important experience in our journey to hold it together.

Senior year will be full of major problems with minor emotional weight like this one and minor problems with major emotional weight. Your child still needs you to set boundaries so they can safely navigate their clumsy efforts at independence. And they need to make mistakes now in order to flourish when those boundaries disappear in a year. The setup you have on your hands is a tricky one, but it makes so much sense. You must parent harder than you ever have, and let go at the same time.

Good talks lower the stress on difficult situations. Here's a good talk template for this time period.

A Talk Template for You and Your High School Senior

Baby [or your favorite sweet name for your person],
As we enter your senior year, we are in new territory, a new phase, a wild period. Soon, you're going to leave home and basically leave your childhood. It makes complete sense if you want more independence this year. It takes practice to make your own decisions and to experience the outcomes of those decisions.

> *I totally understand why you might feel that you have to push against the restrictions I place on you. You have to figure out how to be in this world without me. It's your job!*
>
> *I hate to even admit this because I always want to be your person. I always want to take care of you. It's super hard to let go when my life literally has been dedicated to ensuring your protection. But I know you can handle things! You have built up so many amazing skills. I trust you! And it is still my job to parent you. I'm not letting go quite yet. Senior year is hard. It wouldn't be right for me to release you right as things hit their trickiest.*
>
> *So, this next ten or eleven months will be kind of complicated. It's your job to push away and my job to hold on. We're in a not-quite-yet phase of independence. We won't always get it right. Sometimes I'll be overprotective, and sometimes you'll want more freedom than I can give. So you will push and I will pull, and we will have conflicts.*
>
> *I want you to know that, as we hit the big and little disagreements of this phase, I recognize the friction as a sign that we are both doing the right thing. This is the way it's supposed to be. I am so proud of you!*
>
> *I love you so much!*

As you negotiate senior year, you also need to collaborate on this little project of next steps, and I assume, since you're reading this, you'll need to collaborate on college applications. Applying to college is no joke. If you are feeling stressed, pat yourself on the back. You are showing that you care. Even though you are probably worried that the process isn't further along (nearly all parents are), there is still plenty of time. It's okay if your student still seems miles from their essay.

There are a couple of important things that have to happen quickly, though. Bribery might be effective.

Suggest Letter Writers

Your student needs to request letters from two teachers and their counselor. Ask them if they need help thinking about letter writers. If you know their teachers, you might suggest a few who you love: "I love Ms. Winchester; she might be great because . . . ." This phrasing tends to work better than, "You should pick Ms. Winchester."

If you don't know your person's teachers, ask them about their teachers: "I'm sorry, but I just realized that I don't know a single one of your teachers! Can you walk me through your classes and tell me about each of them? Here, sit down. I just bought some cookies. And made tea. And invited a support puppy over. I won't be too pushy or weird. I promise."

Your kid might act like they're ignoring you. They might really want to do this on their own. They may want to show you how capable they are. But they also may be grateful for your suggestions and your collaboration because they might be feeling quite unsure.

Build Some Resumes

You may have a killer job and a satisfying career. You may be coasting and content. That's wonderful. Maybe you've never created a resume, never needed a resume, never wanted a resume. Regardless, now might be a decent time to assemble your skills and hold them in your head, on your computer, or on paper.

Having your kid leave home can change the shape of you, your time, and your passions. Watching them go through the process, in all its wildness and sweetness, is inspiring. As your young person launches themselves into dreams that seem to magically materialize, you can, too, in big and little ways. You might find a new job, consider a shift in the way you do things at work, go back to school, ask for a promotion, retire, start a side business, or return to work after a break.

If you've stepped aside from the professional sphere to participate in the most ridiculously undervalued position in the world, parenthood, vow that you are going to find someone to pay you money, cash, dollars. Remind yourself that you have been accumulating critical experience for the last eighteen years and that you would be a catch for any organization or company out there. Consider your caretaking, your editing, your contemplating, and your decision-making, leading, following, listening, diagnosing, emergency management, social work genius. Value those skills. Make a resume.

Revisiting a resume or making a resume might be a poignant way not only to consider your present moment but also to connect with your student. They are at an early point in their path and could use your practical tips and wise suggestions.

Offer Help to Your Child as They Write Their Teacher Emails

Although I have provided some very specific instructions earlier in the chapter for your young person, they may not read them. They may be scared and avoidant. If they are stuck, the best way to help them write their teachers is to sit beside them with your body between their chair and the door so they are trapped. Then go through the steps. Stay until they click the "Send" button. They will feel so much better when they are done with this step—the official beginning of things. The relief will help them forgive you for your pushiness.

Also this is your first official test of helpfulness. Put on your most patient, kind, complimentary, helpful self.

Ask If Your Student Has Met with Their Teachers and Counselor

When you say, "Hey, did you check in with Ms. Winchester about the letter?," your person might share a long story about the interaction with Ms. Winchester and their glee over her consent and her kindness. This is amazing! You are stepping through the process. Relief! Joy!

But your student might not share an epic story. They might say, "Yeah." When you ask a follow-up question, "So will she write a letter for you?" they might respond, "Yeah." At this point, you won't know if your student did check in or if they didn't check in. They might be putting you off because they may have forgotten. Or maybe they did, but the emotion was a lot and it's too much to share. Or maybe it went badly. Maybe the teacher agreed to write a letter but didn't seem excited. You just don't know.

You have a unique opportunity in this uncertain moment. You have the opportunity to believe. Belief is so hopeful. "Oh, that's wonderful, honey! I am so proud of you for taking that step." Believe it, with your whole heart, that they did take that step. Otherwise what are your options, really?

I became very paranoid as my teenagers progressed through high school. There were so many difficult situations that they might encounter. So many opportunities for untruth—lies that would protect them and me. I wanted to know all the details of every situation. I wanted to have control as things became potentially even dangerous. But often, I just couldn't have control. I couldn't force stories, and if I did, those stories wouldn't give me power to retroactively fix them.

When I was teaching college, students would occasionally present me with family deaths that caused late papers. I would wonder about the truth of these situations. But what is one to do with a family death? A possible lie? We can't control this situation. We can't force truth or admission or learning. We can just empathize with that death. We can teach and share kindness. "I am so, so sorry about your uncle. Please pass my love on to your family." Because, sometimes, uncles really do die. And it is really sad.

Your best option in questionable situations is belief. If you believe, you will show your child that you have faith in them. If your faith is misplaced, your student will want to put it right. And they will check in with Ms. Winchester. It is a lovely thing to believe, to have faith, to have hope.

Celebrate Those Letter Requests

Celebrate every little piece of this process. Remember to tell your kid how proud you are. Remember to recognize how challenging these little steps can be. Remember to acknowledge all the tiny swirling bits that must link together to make things happen. Celebrate with ice cream or happiness or a hug.

Celebrate yourself, especially if they completely ignore your efforts. Remember, they're doing their job. They are trying to leave you with as much grace as they can muster. You are so patient and good!

Check in about Future SAT and ACT Tests

You know how far and how hard to push your student. If they seem unsure about whether to retake the tests, and if you have money to cover the fee or time to apply for a fee waiver, suggest that they just give it a shot. If they are done, they're done. It's okay. No regrets!

WEEK 3, SEPTEMBER 6–12

WAIT, WHO AM I?

IT'S PRETTY EASY TO LOSE YOURSELF IN THE PROCESS OF BECOMing yourself. Students, I bet you just want to sit down and write a fabulous college essay really quick, something catchy and clever that represents you perfectly. I bet you can feel it in your head, announcing itself. Maybe you've even tried to sit down and write it out a couple of times, but that catchy, clever thing eludes you. And you find yourself scrolling or snacking, waiting for it to come back. You might be at the point when you start to doubt that the catchy clever thing ever existed at all. Maybe you have absolutely nothing to say. Maybe you've never done anything and never been anyone? That catchy, clever thing was a lie!

Truth is, you're right. And wrong. The different parts of you that were to constitute your phenomenal essay were bouncing back and forth around in your brain, making you *think* they were an organized little packet of essay-like images and arguments. But those thoughts aren't an organized little packet. You have to do the organizing through writing. The catchy, clever thing doesn't exist. You have to do work to get it on paper. But you exist. And you have moved your body and mind through time in a way that is entirely unique. There is so much potential for catchy and clever and warm and funny and poignant and ambitious and delightful. It just takes a little work and some patience.

STUDENTS
Write Three Lists That You Save Forever

Record twenty things that you love, twenty things that happened to you, and twenty things that are important to you on your computer or in a nice notebook. If you get stuck, go through your senses: What do you like to see, smell, taste, listen to, or feel? Look through pictures on your phone and in your family photo albums. Mentally run through your years in school. Be specific and expansive. If you write down music, write down what type of music, your favorite album, whether you like to dance to it or cry to it. How does the music move through your head and shift your thoughts? If you love your iguana, what do you love about it? What do you hate about it? Do you like to feed it bugs? I always thought that would be hard. Don't censor yourself. Be free to be long, short, or entirely tangential.

If it's easy for you to get to sixty things, add another twenty. If you are completely stuck at five, just start including the favorite part of your outfit today. The best thing that happened to you today. The worst thing that happened to you today. Then do the same thing for last Wednesday. Nothing is too trivial or too common.

Include things like Hot Cheetos, the color green, and your sauté pan when considering "things that you love." When you think about "things that happened," include the big, the small, the good, and the bad: your sister's wedding shower, the long months of grief, that time you went to Dunkin' with your friend, a failed test, talking to your aunt's parrot, learning a new trick with your yo-yo, or breaking your wrist or your computer. "Important things" might include honesty, a frugal life style, living for the moment, family gatherings, the smell of coconut, time with your cat, or a particular memory. Don't worry too much about categories or wording. Just get the ideas from your heart, your gut, and your head onto paper.

Sixty is a lot. But you could probably do a thousand. There are so many little moments that matter. These lists help you gather and save the feelings, ideas, and things as if you were building a little treasure chest of you. Creating the lists helps you remember who you are. The more items you write down, the more easily you'll be able to see the shape of you. In this life of so-much-information, so-much-to-do, we tend to discount our everyday things, the random beauty, and our idiosyncratic desires. We might even discount our stories, our loves, and our despair as obstacles to productivity. But our lists and their particular conglomerations are unique. Totally unique. And special. These details fill great essays.

Share Your Lists with the People You Love
I asked your adults to make lists, too, about themselves. Compare lists. Have your friends make lists and compare your lists with theirs, too. It's kind of cool how our brains form with one another, for better or worse. We can't help but shape ourselves around others, in distinction or conjunction. Longtime couples even begin to look like each other. We are these adorable little mimics who do what we see, so our face muscles morph us to look similar to the people in our sight lines. Our neural pathways etch themselves with our persistent patterns of behavior. If we become unsteady when we get a flu shot, our hearts might race at the scent of an alcohol wipe even when there is no needle for miles. If our heart races every time we see a particular person, we may find our heart fluttering to slouchy jeans, amber cologne notes, and drum riffs. Our brains know our connections and formulate us spectacularly. So those people who connect with you might feel the world as you do. Their lists might have striking similarities and absolute differences. They might love things that you have decided to hate. They might love things that you forgot about loving.

Add onto your lists with your people. Think about your lists with music. Add to them as you run, shower, or lay down for bed at night. You have such an amazing set of perceptions, experiences, and memories. Your world overflows.

Acknowledge That You Will Be Stepping Away

You will be moving away from those humans who have cared for you and known you for such a long time. Even if you don't plan to leave home in this next phase of your life, you will probably enter into a phase of greater independence. It's bittersweet, right? You don't have to say anything to these people if you don't want, but it's kind of nice to get into a habit of acknowledging and honoring feelings. The more you acknowledge and honor, the more you feel. And life is a good thing to feel.

Consider Your Future

Now that you've considered your life and your identity for a bit, how might your fantastic self and your dreamy characteristics unfold through time? What do you want to be when you grow up? Write it down.

Do you know? Some people do. They just know they are destined to be a ceramicist, a dermatologist, a union activist, a financier. Their life has delivered them onto a particular doorstep, through talent, through practice, through a persistent dream. If you know, fantastic! Honor that dream. Also, tell your dream that you are open to its changing shape as time goes on.

When you are young, there's so much you still don't know. When you are old, there's so much you still don't know. You don't have to stay on any one path, even if it feels immutable. It's perfectly okay and often the way of the present world to take a meandering path through time. Rather than considering a switching, turning, reversing direction as problematic, it might be useful to think of your future as a journey of skill building where change brings you new talents and visions. These new skills and this new knowledge help you more adeptly address the sticky problems of the world and contribute to its beauty.

I encourage you to pick a path confidently because it doesn't and shouldn't be perfect or forever. It only must help you learn and become a better person. So if you have no idea about your future path, that's great. Let's do this!

Pick a few things and try them on. When you shop for clothes, you might see something on a hanger and be curious about it. When you put it on in the dressing room, with a slimming mirror or fluorescent lighting, you might feel different about it. If you walk around in it and catch your reflection, you can become suddenly confident, or you might feel silly. The cloth might soften or wrinkle or irritate. You have to try stuff on and walk around with it for a bit.

Try on some vocations, careers, and activities that might be cool. What do people say you'd be good at? What ideas float around in the back of your head? What school subjects feel comfortable, fun, challenging, inspiring? Write a few down along with your beautiful lists. Tell people about them. When you tell people about your interests, you are trying them on. How do they feel?

What Would You Do in the Movie Version of Your Life?

Think about the most preposterous thing that you can imagine yourself doing. Who might you be in your wildest dreams? Write that down. Even if you're the practical sort, even if everyone has always told you what you're destined to become, it's interesting to consider life at your most audacious. Do you want to be a professional ping-pong player? Or a mermaid? These vocations might be impractical with regard to your skill set. But just the act of considering such possibilities shifts your brain into a creative mode.

What if you could study the history of mermaid-like creatures—the huldra in Norse mythology or the siren in Greek mythology? What if you became an expert in underwater creature songs? You could record whale songs off the side of a boat in Alaska after your junior year! Would you like to use sports for peace negotiation? Are you curious about the chemical composition of the bumpy rubber ping-pong surfaces? You might find a potential direction by following your passion. Critically, you must uncover your weirdness to find your unique beauty. And practically speaking, the more unique your plan, the catchier your application. Write down *ping-pong player*. Write down *mermaid*.

Combine Your Audacious Dream with the More Practical One

Figure out the intersections of the thing you think you're supposed to be and the thing that would be odd and amazing. This combination might help you become more specific in your interests. If you feel like you should be a scientist and you love music, why not be a scientist who studies sound waves? Or an ethnomusicologist? Consider elaborating on this in a college essay.

Writing a college application isn't really about compiling the "who" that you know now—a clarinet player, a soccer goalie, a kid currently fighting with parents, a decent student, a good test taker, a senior with an okay boyfriend. But it is about finding the seed that you know, and speculating on what flower it might become.

The ability to speculate is a crucial skill not only for your applications but also for your scholarship proposals, your future jobs, your best life. You must cultivate the ability to say you know something when you still have very little idea. Every time you apply for a job or a grant, you have to release a vision of how you might perform, of how you would find contentment in a particular position. You have to act like you know, when of course you don't. It is not dishonest or wrong to say that you are going to be a veterinarian, an anthropologist, or a criminologist when you still aren't sure what those words even mean. It's astute and good practice to speculate and dream into the unknown. And again, you can *always* change your mind.

An exception: There are some colleges and programs that have stickier commitments. You might need to apply to an engineering program at a particular college, for example, if you want to be on the engineering track within that particular college. Gauge your desire and your abilities and go for it. It's easier to leave selective programs than it is to enter them, so you might need to make a decision before you apply, in these cases. But still, you can shift. You can always shift.

Visit College Websites

While there, immerse yourself in the possibilities for your future. Write to the most interesting person you find. Tab through the university website seeking these words: *Academics, Courses of Study, Undergraduate Majors and Concentrations, Degree Programs, Undergraduate Degrees, Undergraduate Programs, Majors and Minors.* Every website is a bit different, but eventually, using these words, you will find a long list of things to study: *African studies, anthropology, applied mathematics, Arabic, architecture.* . . . The lists are often alphabetized. Click on the programs, majors, and departments that pique your interest. Find a list of professors within those departments. Read their bios. Do a search for them on the internet. Consider their lives.

You will likely find fascinating people who do amazing things. Write to at least one of these people. Look, their email address is right there! Type it into an email. You don't need to be impressive. Just be curious. Ask questions. "Dear Dr. Chrysanthemum, My name is Jill Constantino and I am a prospective student. I am absolutely fascinated with your work. [Here, you can tell them briefly why you're fascinated. Then . . .] I wondered if you might answer a couple of quick questions." This activity is good email writing practice (see week 2 for more tips). At worst, they don't write you back, but you have practiced an important skill. But more likely, the conversation will be inspiring—maybe even life shaping. And though you shouldn't depend on this, once in a while, professors contact their friends in admissions to advocate for curious students.

Regardless of whether anything happens with your email, you can and should write about your fascination with this particular professor in the "Why this university?" essay. More on this later.

CONCERNED ADULTS

Write Three Lists

Record twenty things that you love, twenty things that happened to you, and twenty things that are important to you. Your student is doing this, too. Check out the beginning of this chapter for more thorough directions.

Having raised a child and sifted your entire life through their well-being, you may find yourself suddenly struggling to locate your autonomy, your identity. Do you remember who you are? I bet you do. Let's assume those little bits of you are tucked in some recess of your brain behind the old Cheerios and anxiety. Write them all down.

Compare Your Lists with Your Student's Lists

Often, these little lists are so lovely that they want to be shared. If you offer yours up, vulnerability can happen. Vulnerability is the best thing you can give your baby. They need your softness and openness so that they can give you their softness and openness. It's scary and beautiful.

You can also help them add to their list. You can remind them of the details in their items, so that they may fill out their ideas. You know your person in ways that they might be too insecure to appreciate yet. You might remember things about them from when they were little, aspects of their personality that have persisted through time—so long that they have become the hum of the universe. You can point out that hum so they can appreciate its song.

Research Colleges and Their Qualities

You may have started looking at colleges a decade ago, driving through them and appreciating their flower beds and beautiful stone facades. You might know the six colleges within an hour radius that will work fine. You might feel that your child must go to an Ivy League or a Big Ten school (I think there are eighteen of them as of this writing). Fantastic.

It's also okay if you're still bewildered by the whole concept of making a college list. In any case, it's worth looking further into things. You might start with books and websites. Here are a few: *Fiske Guide to Colleges, Colleges That Change Lives, U.S. News & World Report College Rankings,* or *The Princeton Review: The Best 390 Colleges.*

Research the programs that interest your child. If your child has spent a childhood considering the relative value of trading cards like baseball or Pokémon, look up "best college economics programs." If you have a lifeguard who finds herself oddly interested in the precise balance of pool chemicals necessary to keep pee nontoxic, you might search "best chemistry programs." If they take apart your electronics or build dams in your stream, key in "best engineering schools." If they love to argue, sculpting words around their thoughts, think "best journalism college," "best political science undergraduate program," "best philosophy thinkers and their universities," "what is comparative literature?"

You may have a child who will eat this activity up, mark up books, dive into websites, and make a map for your next road trip. Support this eagerness. Buy multicolored Post-its. Make them a smoothie. Give them a protein shake. Brew some tea or kombucha.

Conversely, your child might be utterly disinterested in or terrified by such an activity. In either case, it's good to start the conversation about what colleges exist, which elements they contain, and what type of life they might provide.

The guidebooks make this easy for you. *Fiske* gives star ratings for academics, social life, and quality of life. The write-ups will give you a sense for urban/rural, student body diversity, community size, and living environment. The guides and the internet provide GPA and standardized test ranges for acceptance rates so you can engage the foggiest notions of likelihood.

This week, just peruse. Start thinking about weekends and little car trips. Consider places that would make a lovely Sunday adventure. Wonder if your favorite clothing store might be on one of the avenues off of one of the campuses. Consider buying yourself a cute sweater, maybe something colorful.

Make Your Life Better

Hey, how are things? Are you good? Are you happy with how your body feels? Do you sleep okay? Are you feeling fuzzy or anxious? There are so many things you might do to bring some fresh air into your own life. Could you make a doctor's appointment you've been avoiding? What about giving up alcohol for a month, or making a Manhattan every Friday evening at 5 p.m. to mark the end of the work week? Do you want to start cooking some vegetarian dishes? Are you interested in watching award-winning movies? Do you fancy reading books that would make your former English teacher proud? Now is a decent time to trade in child-rearing anxieties for something healthy and happy.

Do Some Fun Things

As your kid is doing very grown up and hard things, consider doing something young, weird, or decadent with them. If you can't get them to play along, go by yourself! Feel joy and spread it!

An Odd List of Indulgences for You and Your Person

- Find a stream. Throw some rocks in. See if you can skip them. See how many skips you can get.
- Plant herbs—basil, oregano, thyme, mint. Put the seeds in a window in little pots. The terracotta ones look cute, but don't get hung up. Use anything! Grow a lot, even if it feels like a stupid amount. Abundance.
- Go to a museum you've never explored. Agree to tilt your heads when you look at an item. Try to notice if other people are noticing you tilting your head.
- Buy the most expensive, decadent butter you have ever seen and spread it on a baguette or a piece of bakery bread, toasted. Maybe even sprinkle some salt crystals on it—fancy salt with big crystals, if possible. Or you could spread Nutella, if you find butter boring.
- Look at the clouds for a while.
- Agree to tell a funny personal story to someone you've just met, a little bit before that sort of sharing feels appropriate. Like your waiter when you're out for lunch or the oil change person when you're helping your child remember to change the oil. (I burned out the most adorable 1980 Volvo station wagon.)
- Find frogs and pick them up. Hold them low to the ground, though, so they don't get hurt. This will probably have to wait for spring. There's time.
- Smell flowers, anywhere—open field, botanical garden, Costco.
- Paint together—watercolor, oil, finger paint. On your table, in the garage, at a painting place, plein air.
- Make a smoothie with at least six ingredients. Here is one that I love but you might hate: carrots, ginger, apple, lemon, banana, turmeric, chia, flax, cayenne, a little water, and

- some ice. Put in a ton of ginger and cayenne so it almost makes you choke.
- Find a wild animal. Watch it as if Jane Goodall were standing next to you. Squirrels and ants count.
- The next time you see a really, really fancy car and strangers are taking pictures of it, walk up to the driver-side door, go for the handle (but don't really touch it because you might set off an alarm). Glare at the people taking pictures. Then tell them that you're kidding. It's so funny!
- Get a thing of bubbles when you go to the grocery store and blow them out your car window, if you can do it without modeling distracted driving. Or use them when you get home, in the kitchen, if that feels more comfortable. Maybe buy the kits that make giant bubbles. Really go for it. Or Orbeez!
- Try to imagine what aliens look like. Think super broadly outside of any *Star Wars* preconceptions. Hope that we find some in our lifetimes.
- Get a decadent bar of chocolate for dessert one night. It should be expensive. Eat it slowly with red wine, coffee, or milk.
- Leave messages in library books. This always happens in movies but never in real life—not in my real life yet, anyway. Give it a shot. Give it ten shots.
- Moo at cows.
- Yell "Marco" in a grocery store. Like in Marco Polo—the game you play in the pool.
- Go for a cliché walk in the rain. You could even wear boots and splash in puddles.
- Go outside during a lightning storm but don't hold anything metal. And make sure you're shorter than the stuff around you.
- Lie down on hot cement. Feel the warmth on the back of your arms and legs. Maybe in the summer or on vacation.
- Shop for matching clothing that makes you both feel cool—like a T-shirt or skater shoes or sunglasses or a hat.

- Run a road race. Throw your arms into the air when you cross the finish line. Maybe drop to your knees and put your head in your hands. Feel glory, even if you both are super slow.
- Go on a picnic. If you have one of those wicker baskets with compartments, great!
- Buy a Slurpee. If you do get the Slurpee, put the lid on first (the rounded lids, not the flat ones) and don't overfill! I know you think you remember how to fill a Slurpee cup, but you don't, and it will be a huge mess and you'll have to decide whether to talk to the person at the counter about the mess you made. (I don't think you need to.) But you do have the power to avoid this whole scenario by using appropriate lid strategies.
- Lie on the edge of a boat or dock so your face is hanging over into the water. Look at the water for a long time, like at least three minutes, and imagine that a shark is going to come up and eat your face.

Suspend Money Worries

We'll consider the scary expenses regularly in this book, but right now, your job is to suspend the worry so it stays out of the way of brainstorming. Sending a kid to college is so expensive! There are some things you can do about this, and many that are out of your control. We'll work through it the best we can.

Having a child is also prohibitively expensive. No one would ever do it if they considered the expense. It's inconceivable. But you had that child and you've made it to this point. And even if "I wouldn't change a thing," has a begrudging edge to it at this point, I bet your life is so full—full of not only complexity and struggle but also learning and gratitude, a conglomeration of experiences and emotions that lead to no regrets.

Maybe it is a bit stressful. Certainly, it is all stressful. We will mitigate this college stress to the best of our abilities in order to find you a place of no regrets. College costs are not straightforward. Schools that look expensive might be quite cheap. Schools that seem inexpensive might be pricier. Avoid big decisions until you know a little more. Just keep stepping, my friend.

Go to FAFSA and Read

Consider filing for Federal Student Aid (https://studentaid.gov/announcements-events/fafsa-support). Everyone should, actually. There is no income limit for eligibility. The deadlines and specifics change year to year. Get on this as early as you can.

Even if you are very, very, very rich, it is nice to contemplate the process and to consider the expenses. If you are kind of rich, you might still qualify for money, especially if you are applying to top-50 schools. Almost all of the top-tier institutions offer need-based money, and because these schools tend to be quite expensive before grants, scholarships, and aid, they know that you might need the money even if you have some money. Most don't want to break you, really. If you have very little money, the shiniest and most expensive schools might be your cheapest bet. If your kid has the grades, make sure they aim high!

Week 4, September 13–19

WHERE AM I GOING?

Dear students, you have two tasks for this week. They involve a type of focus that may feel unfamiliar. It's a close-in, open-eyed absorption that you must engage in, while fuzzing out everything else around you—your future, the past, homework, obligations, abilities, possibilities, responsibilities, insecurities. Fuzz them all out.

Picture a little green frog, shiny and adorable. It's sitting in a shallow puddle. Then it jumps from that puddle into the air and splashes down into a sweet pond surrounded by trees. It swims up to a log in the sun and is perfectly content. Watch that frog in your head for a minute. It is so full of simple movement and beauty that it just makes you happy. I want this focus for you this week. I want you to connect with this way of looking at the pictures in your head while feeling the emotions they evoke. And I want you to connect with your own process of hopping freely about. I hope you feel free and beautiful as you write. I want you to be able to imagine your little frogness in a moment of time—not projected through ambition or anxiety, future or past.

When you're writing, focus only on the stuff that makes you adorable. It might seem complicated to find your adorable. You might be thinking, *Nah, you got the wrong kid.* But I don't. And more, I bet that I could find your adorable (maybe blissfully adorable, heartbreakingly adorable, hilariously adorable, or quietly adorable) in every single story you tell, as long as you tell it with enough detail. It's the simplest thing in the world to grab onto your you-ness, see it in your head, and write your insides, your gut, your heart, your spirit, your core onto a page. But it's also the hardest.

Writing can make you cry. It can confuse you and incite ridiculous fights over things like facial expressions or dirty socks. It is one of the great mysteries of the world, why writing can make one feel so upset. You've heard people talk about writer's block. It's nothing special. It's not reserved for "real" writers or "good" writers. It's just that space between *I'm-the-dumbest-person-in-the-world-and-no-one-likes-me/I-hate-everyone* and *Oh, there we go, my first draft. Nice.* For your first task this week, you will write that draft. And that draft will be atrocious. More on this atrociousness in a minute.

Your other task requires no major freakouts, but it might feel hard for you to blur out the world while you do it. It might feel overwhelming. You will begin a tentative, changeable, you-are-not-locked-into-anything list of schools to which you might apply. When you're listing, I want you to flit about, ignoring the anxiety, responsibility, and time pressure to get things just right. This list of yours says everything and nothing about your future. You might apply to all of the schools or only a few of the schools. You might get into all of the ones you love or none of them. It doesn't matter yet. You are just figuring out what you like; you are figuring out what might make you feel like that little frog—free and happy. So, again, you're going to have to trust your gut and your heart as you feel for a place.

Also, you need this list because you need to figure out when you have to finish your applications. It's good to have exact dates in your vision. They can feel looming, but they can also feel definitive, concrete, and calming.

STUDENTS
Write a Truly Atrocious First Draft for Your Principal Essay

All great writing must start with not-great writing. We really can't skip the not-great, as much as we'd love to. Writing becomes better and better as we rethink, as we push off our original thoughts into the deeper, more vibrant, and more complex. You have to do this first awful draft. In *Bird by Bird* (1994), Anne Lamott coins the phrase "shitty first drafts" when she describes how important these horrible little scratches of writing are. Bad writing allows for freedom, which is necessary to produce beauty. Your awful draft will bring calm as it opens the doors of your brain so you can get this application done.

Give yourself an hour, two at the max. Make sure you get 650 words down onto your computer screen or a piece of paper. The word limit for the Common App essay is 650. The limit is different for other essay questions (your supplementals) and applications (the UC Application, as one example), which require fewer words. It doesn't matter. You just need to write—as much as you can, as fast as you can. Do you know when you write best? I am amazing before noon. Everything I put down is stunningly evocative and compelling if I write it before noon. After noon, I am a complete idiot. I don't write well in a dirty room. Though, somehow, I write really well on the floor of a hallway and also in the driver's seat of my car (when it's not moving and the seat is pushed back). I like things to be quiet. Consider when, where, and how you write best and try to meet those conditions. No one set of conditions is better than any other. Knowing your ideal writing conditions will help you as you write throughout your life.

But on this draft, it doesn't matter if your conditions suck because you are going to suck. So, pick a window of time after which you *must* leave your house for something amazing. Or start writing one or two hours before an important obligation. Having an end deadline will help you not mess around too much before you start. Don't let yourself leave until you have completely filled a page with single-spaced 12-point font. I like *Times New Roman*. Make a deal with someone to dunk your phone in the toilet if you don't get 650 words down in that small window of time. Make them promise that they will hold you to your deadline, then write like crazy. Even if you have to repeat words and sentences to arrive at your word count within the allotted time (like Jack Nicholson in *The Shining*, "All work and no play ..."), do it. If you meet your goal and you're on fire, keep going. Don't worry about the essay prompts. Don't even look at them. They will get in your way. The prompts are general enough that anything you write will fit. I promise.

Pick Images, Stories, and Ideas from Your Lists for Your Draft

You might write one story that contains several items from your list, write several stories about one item, or write several stories about several items. These vignettes will certainly have parallels and potential for integration. Pick something that you can see in your brain, to start. Are you looking at a window? "The window has a painted blue frame." Do you see your brother? Is he standing next to a broken pot? "My brother is standing on our black-and-white-checkered floor, next to a broken pot." Pictures are great to write with because they move through space and memories with contingency. One thing touches another that touches another in your memory, carrying you through time and emotion. "There was a broken thing. It was on the floor connected to a wall with a window. My mom was looking in that window, with a rake in her hand. That rake was left in our farm shed by the previous owners. When those owners died in a tornado that blew through our town, the farm was quite wrecked." The contingencies force your writing. Don't worry about good; just follow your picture with lots of words.

Stories are also helpful to write with because they move through time in order. The chronology helps you write your next sentence. "I threw the phone at my brother. As I was beginning to feel shame, he stood up with my mom's antique pot in his hand and lunged over the couch. Conflicts like this were more frequent after my uncle passed away."

If you get stuck when you are writing, consider your senses. Write about the color, sound, smell, taste, and feel of your subject matter. "When my brother launched his short little legs over the tattered couch, time froze. The smell of leaves wafted through the open window and distracted me." The more your reviewer can feel, smell, taste, and touch what you experienced, the more you will hold their interest, and the more they will want you to build interest in others at their school!

You have two goals with your essay: (1) keep your reviewer interested, and (2) let them hold the intricacies of fabulous you. You need to authentically shine, but you don't want to show off, act entitled, or demonstrate a lack of self-awareness. It is a complicated genre! It is perfectly reasonable for your first draft to be atrocious. But bad can turn great fairly quickly. Here is a look at the drafting process through two examples.

Examples of the Rough Draft to Final Draft Progression

Example 1: A student of mine has a fantastic grandma. (Not a great principal topic because it's kind of common to have a fantastic grandma.) That great grandma taught her to sew. (Closer to something unique, but still in the realm of millions of people. She's using two items from her list. Draft 1.) The grandma taught her to sew in Spanish when she couldn't quite speak the language yet. (Lovely, three items. Draft 2.) And her young feminist self was skeptical at first, due to the gendered nature of sewing. (Yes, yes! Draft 3.) But she liked adapting patterns and making her own prototypes. (Great word for an aspiring engineer!) And this whole process of prototyping can also be found in the activist work that she and her mom do. (We're really getting somewhere now! More items from her list. Draft 4.) Come to think of it, there are generations of bad-ass women that she has followed in becoming her bad-ass self who prototypes models of materials and mass movements. And more, she wants to make prototypes for the medical industry that might solve small material problems as well as larger social justice ones. (Bam! Draft 5.) You can find this essay on page 185, "Essay 1, Final."

Example 2: Here's another real-student essay process that shifted quickly from the general to the specific by incorporating several disparate topics from her lists. She started with a broad idea: "I love numbers!" (Too broad, right?) But she had some specific reasons why numbers make her comfortable—the quantitative is solid and certain; numbers give a sense of security. She illustrated this with an example of a favorite equation. (This was draft 1.) In the next draft, she picked a story from her life she thought she'd like to tell, but she wasn't sure how it was connected: "I once painted the number 14 on a baby turtle as part of a conservation project." After brainstorming, she realized she felt a similar comfort holding onto that turtle as she feels when she works with numbers, security. Numbers and turtles help her make space and time concrete. (Draft 2.) Not until draft 3 did she realize she was talking about a particular type of belonging. Through very different experiences and ideas in her life, she found a coherence. You can find this essay on page 187, "Essay 2, Final."

WHERE AM I GOING?

Focus on Something Tiny, Then Expand into Your Bigger Ideas

Start itty bitty! Minuscule! If you were to describe your body, you might say that you are blah blah tall and you weigh blah blah pounds and you have blah blah hair and eyes and a nose. Chances are, this writing about your body might not be very interesting because many people would use these same parameters to describe something that is pretty common. But, if you were to describe a scar on your body or a unique and odd function of one tiny part of your body, or a dream you had about your belly button, we might be getting somewhere. If you are writing about something many people write about (sports, a friend, your grandparents), make sure your angle is incredibly unique and focused on you and your own characteristics!

You may have scored the most amazing basket, line-drive, backflip, computer program, or family member, but your essay must be about how those scores messed up a friendship, broke your coach's elbow, or reflected off the pavement in a pattern so beautiful you became fixated for six hours and someone had to bring you cinnamon toast as dusk was coming on because they were worried about the coyotes getting you.

> ### **An Example of Focusing Tiny**
>
> I had a student who was very good at a cool video game in which you use Google Street View to pinpoint locations on Earth (*GeoGuessr*—you must try this game!). Rather than start his essay with a description of the game (which might seem narrow enough), he went deep into the play. One time, he spent a whole night studying telephone poles because he found that the particular structures of telephone poles contained great information about their locations. Through this process of studying telephone

poles, he also learned a lot about colonization patterns. So, his essay literally starts with a close-in description of the concrete holes in telephone poles. He didn't even know why he found them so captivating until he started writing. You can find this essay on page 189, "Essay 3, Final."

Be Humble and Self-Aware

When you write your principal and supplemental essays, you must write everything you know about yourself, while simultaneously uncovering all that you don't know.

Recognize Your Privilege

As you pick your topics, recognize your privilege. Privilege doesn't mean just economic advantages or masculine edge, though these are types of privilege. We all have some form of privilege. We might have bodies that work well with the systems of our country and our governments. We might have ideas that track along the hegemonic pathways—those ways that are considered "normal." We might have two loving parents in our lives. Our native language might be the same as the language that is spoken in school. Maybe our house is stocked with books and food. Acknowledge your good economic fortune, cultural ease, athletic ability, or social mastery, but avoid any superiority connected to it.

Be Curious about All You Don't Know

Don't be cliché as you recognize your privilege. If you participated in some amazing volunteer project and realized, in the end, that "they didn't need me as much as I needed them," take it a step further. This "they didn't need me . . ." thing is a cliché that makes its way into so many college essays. To take it further, you might wonder to yourself in writing: *How did my life wait so long to teach me the lessons of that service project? How did social and cultural power play into the communications and relationships of the project? Who carried power when and how? Were those lessons I learned the right ones? How was I unaware, unsure, or even problematic? How am I still unaware, unsure, or even problematic?*

Be curious about your transforming situation in the world, no matter who you are! You will not fully understand someone's culture/religion/identity/intellectual stance because you had a class with them, did a service project with them, or became friends with them. Keep wondering in your head and in your writing. Humility is key, and curiosity opens your brain to marvelous self-exploration. Questions can be so much lovelier than answers. Ask honest questions instead of giving uncertain answers whenever you find yourself speculating. There are many supplemental essays trying to assess your openness, your humility, your ability to learn, and your capacity for respect and empathy as you interact with those who are different than you. Show that you are eager to learn and eager to share, if you are. If you aren't that into empathy, respect, or learning, give it a shot, for yourself and for the world.

Shout Out Your Unique Ways of Being!
Shout out as strong and as proud as you can! In general, schools need people who have a wide range of experiences, ways of thinking, ways of processing, ways of interacting with the world. It is responsible, self-respecting, and helpful to write about your own identity—your culture, your race, your religion, your gender, your sexual orientation, your body shape, your abilities. Show how your particular formation of self has equipped you to solve problems. College is all about finding the holes in knowledge and filling them; colleges want to solve the problems of the world. You might have skills that others don't! Your different abilities, different perspectives, and unique positionality may be exactly what a school is looking for as they seek new answers for new and old problems. Celebrate not only your personal uniqueness but also the many forms of humanity that exist!

Take on the Big, Little, Good, Bad, Ugly, and Beautiful
While focusing narrowly will help you write beautifully, you can really write about anything. Some advisors will recommend avoiding political issues, highly personal experiences, volunteer trips, sports, romance, mental health, injuries, and such. But really, no topic is out of bounds! As long as you are nice, self-aware, and thoughtful, the sky's the limit. Don't constrict yourself.

I hope that you don't feel shame or guilt about using a difficult experience. If an experience has shaped you, and you feel comfortable and ready to write about it, do it. I had a student who didn't want to mention her friend's death, though it had the biggest impact on her high school career. She was worried that she would, in some ways, be using the tragedy for her benefit. But you really don't have to evaluate your subject matter like that at this point. Write your life. Just write your life. If something has impacted you, write it.

If you write about hard times, make sure you can show how you moved through those hard times. College can be hard. You might be living on your own for the first time, potentially doing really challenging work. Your college admissions officers will be happy to see how you handle struggle. They love resilience.

If you find it hard to demonstrate resilience on a certain topic, it might not be the right topic. But also it might not be the right time to go to school. We all have doubts about whether we're ready for big change. Consider your particular doubts. Go, if you feel scared but eager. But if you're still in the thick of things and you can't really see out of them and you don't feel too resilient or healthy, be kind to yourself. You can take as much time as you need. College will be there. As you take time, you will grow, you will heal, and you will be more and more ready.

WHERE AM I GOING?

Expect Major Overhauls as You Draft

Appreciate yourself when your writing flows gorgeously, but don't get too frustrated when it's embarrassingly bad. Don't delete. This baby is going to change, change, change, so be at peace with the messiness of the process.

Recognize it when you are killing it, when you spin a lovely few words or when you hit on something that feels true and full. Pause when your writing makes you feel smart or beautiful and then create another few sentences of explanation, depth, or extension. You might have found an important idea or thesis.

Equally, don't get down on yourself if your words feel disappointing. We all drop embarrassing words into the world. Keep even the embarrassing stuff. You can move things to a "horrible writing" document. What feels like junk one day for one essay might feel great tomorrow or in the context of another essay. You might stall out on one topic for your major essay, but it could be perfect for a 250-word supplemental essay. Just keep writing.

Let's Make a College List

After tormenting you with my insistence that you should just write fast and recklessly but also be very careful not to be entitled, cliché, general, shy, or boring, you might be thinking, *Lay off, please. I'm overwhelmed.* I know. It's a lot. If you still haven't started that bad essay, stop where you are. Set a timer for twenty minutes. Write.

There. Good job.

Now, let's make a college list. This is a fun and easy task that might also feel overwhelming at first. You have probably already received a lot of advice about the criteria you should use to find your perfect school: Do you want a big school or little school? Public or private? Which schools fit your family's financial situation? Do you learn best in big classes or little classes? Two-year or four-year? Do you want a rowdy party town, or do you prefer a nerdier nature scene? A rowdy nature scene? Nerdy party school? These questions can be tricky to answer because you might have only known one or two places in your entire life. You aren't going to find perfect answers to the "what type of college are you looking for?" question so you shouldn't worry about a perfect list.

Ask questions of the questions and open your mind to all the possibilities instead. How do you know if you're a city person if you've never been to a city? How do you know that you want a huge college if you come from a high school with five hundred kids—or five thousand? If you're shy or an introvert, would going to a huge school where you might find some anonymity be better, or should you force yourself into quicker-forming relationships with a smaller school? Do you know your potential? Will the school's standards, the average class size, the student body fit your work ethic and ambition and create conditions for growth and knowledge building, or will those standards, class sizes, and students conflict with your wellness priorities?

At this point, who knows?! Really. So keep thinking and wondering. Make a scrappy, meandering, open, long list that follows your intuition. And know that the list will continue to shift until you pick your school.

In the "Concerned Adults" section of the previous chapter, I suggested a book or two that might be helpful. If you have one of these books, super! If you don't have a book that lists colleges, your library probably will. If you don't like books, there are TONS of lists online and many tools that can help you find schools: Appily, BigFuture, College Navigator, College Scorecard, CollegeVine, Corsava, Niche, Peterson's College Discovery Center, *Princeton Review*, *U.S. News & World Report*. Start anywhere and then dive into the schools that are appealing. Many high schools have Naviance software, which can also be useful. Once you find a college that seems amazing, search for "schools like [the one you think is amazing]."

Your counselors can help you add to your list. Again, it's okay if your list is long. Once you know more, you can cut it down.

Don't be blind to your set of abilities or limitations, but don't sell yourself short either. If you haven't topped a 1400 on your SAT and your grade point average is A/Bish, you probably won't get into an Ivy League school. If, however, you have a compelling story that shows you are a resilient beast, you might! In some contexts, those grades and scores demonstrate the ability that these schools are seeking. Admission into top 20 schools is always highly competitive and slightly arbitrary, so no matter who you are, don't count on it. The acceptance rates make it really, really hard for *anyone* to get in. But students do graduate from those schools. If it has always been your dream to go to Princeton, maybe you should try, even if your odds are low, low, low. No regrets, my friend!

It costs money and time to apply, though, so should you apply toward loftier dreams or unsure places? Should you apply to a super wide range to see where the money lands? There's no exact science, but these are some points to consider:

- Through applying, you are building your professional capacity, your ability to follow instructions, and your identity. This process makes you better at the process! Dive in and know that you are becoming a better version of yourself, even if you aren't initially sure about the schools you are selecting.
- If you don't have the money for college application fees, schools offer fee waivers. If you have the ability to pay or the time to secure a waiver, applying broadly may save you money because you will have more financial offers to choose from. Additionally, many amazing schools have no application fee. Look up "best schools with no application fee."
- Applying takes time. With each successive application, however, you have more completed application material to

choose from in creating future applications, so applications get progressively easier.

- The more selective your schools are, the less likely you are to get in, no matter who you are. Applying to all of the top-10 schools but no others is not enough. The odds are just too low. Applying to your favorite tippy-top school and then a bunch of safety schools (schools in which you have a high probability of getting in, where your grades and test scores exceed those of most who get in) and target schools (schools in which your GPA and test scores align with the average range of admitted students, giving you an average shot of getting in) is probably also not enough. If you really want to go to a top-20 school and you have the stamina to try and the statistics to make it possible, give yourself a bunch of chances and apply to a bunch of top schools (along with a bunch of targets and safeties you also love). Your process will be long, but you've been training for this.

- If you don't have the energy, time, ambition, or desire to apply to many schools, step through the applications one at a time. Make sure you hit your favorites early but maybe not first. First pancakes usually aren't as beautiful as the ones that follow. First applications aren't either. As long as you apply to your favorites, it's okay if you push them to later in your process—unless you decide you have to apply to them "early action" or "early decision." More on this later.

- Two-year colleges offer an amazing way to save money and a great step forward in learning. They very well might be the way to go. But don't limit yourself to community college just because you're scared and aren't sure who you are yet. Nearly every student out there feels uncertain. Be brave and throw some applications out to four-year colleges. Why not? Don't rule them out yet. The applications themselves will help you figure some things out. On top of that, four-year colleges offer personal growth that may be harder to find in a two-year commuter college. You might consider a gap year, too, before or after you apply. That year would offer opportunities to save money, to grow, and to see the world before a four-year plan.

- Top schools (and by this, I mean the top 20, the top 50, or the top 200 depending on your academic reach), as defined by lists like the *US News & World Report*, have a lot of money, can be cheaper than anything out there, and offer amazing gifts for your growth. People like to pretend that they're all prestige and no substance, but I don't think this is true. Those schools at the top of algorithmically derived lists really do have good things—good financial aid, good student-teacher ratios, good support systems, internships, travel, lawn spaces!

- But those algorithmically derived lists might be woefully incomplete. Don't dismiss Historically Black Colleges, Tribal Colleges and Universities, or niche schools that don't top the lists. The algorithms that consistently put some schools at the top often miss many great schools, possibly because of bias, or just because they haven't been high on the list before. Administrators at top universities who provide information for the algorithms may rank well-known, previously listed schools high, forgetting about excellent universities out of their radar.

- Schools well beyond the top 20 or the top 200 on these lists can be quite amazing. They may offer something special that fits your particular needs. But more, for better or worse, 80 percent of the professors out there went to 20 percent of the universities, often highly ranked. There are a lot of super smart and accomplished people working at a vast array of universities. Further, the schools down these lists may be less research driven, which means the administrators put less pressure on teachers to publish. Instead, these schools prioritize teaching, thereby creating a better classroom experience for students. No matter where you go, you're likely to find brilliance, beauty, and great opportunities for growth.

Make a long list, put it in a spreadsheet if you're so inclined, and write down the first deadline for each college in a column along the side. You can find these dates quite easily through a general search or with some AI assistance, but double-check them with the college website as you get into things. You'll need to consider early action, early decision, and rolling deadlines soon, but don't worry about that quite yet. Just write down some dates.

There. Now you know how to calibrate your panic. Panic is an effective motivator.

CONCERNED ADULTS
Make Your Person Write Their Rough Draft
Set up perfect conditions with soft blankets, shakes, and plates of grapes. Shift strategies if you encounter resistance. If they don't produce a single-spaced page in an agreed-upon period of time, hide the car keys and steal their phone until they show you a page. You are doing them a favor. Set these parameters ahead of time so that they know you will engage in such stubborn and aggressive boundary setting, out of love. Stay strong!

Breathe
Among overwhelming weeks, this one is particularly overwhelming. School and activities are probably going full blast now, and college is getting closer. Your person realizes that the time has come when they must do the things that they had imagined to be quite easy but are finding to be quite complicated. And they very well might be a mess.

It's going to be tempting and the most comfortable of options, at this point, to give up. You might be following a ball of anxiousness around the house as it bashes into siblings, plans, emotional stability, and general hygiene. If you're finding yourself in the middle of a mess, you might just focus on the cleanup. Kind of like cleaning the kitchen, you'll feel better and understand what to cook, what to buy, and how the world works once things are picked up. Just move through and breathe, focusing on the task at hand. Take care of the collateral damage (siblings, dirty dishes, your emotional comfort) and send your applicant to school. Empathetically roll your eyes at your partner or cat. Figure out where the smells are coming from, remove the offensive items, light a candle.

You are remarkably strong and calm. Look at you, just reading a book, learning some possibilities that might help. Hang in there and try not to stay in your anger too long because it doesn't help that much. Feel free to feel sad. Listen to some sad music. American Music Club and Nina Simone help me dive down into the pain. Or you could channel your rage. Try Alanis Morissette or Rage Against the Machine! There is a whole world of gorgeous and powerful emotion out there, just ready to keep you company.

Call a friend with an equally ridiculous child.

Write Your Own College List for Your Student

If they like to do this sort of thing with you, do it together. If they don't want you entering into the process, don't share your list. Yet. Or maybe ever. But it's so helpful to know the worlds that they are considering. They probably will need your help because there is so much information to sift through. And if you will be paying for their college, you have a right to discuss their economic options. If they are paying, information will help you to help them figure out debt, its graciousness, and its dangerous grip. Talking openly and empathetically about money before, during, and after the application process is crucial. But for now, keep the money conversations general and in a "let's see" place.

As tyrannical as you were with your rough draft commands, be relaxed and open about first college lists. Hopefully, your college applicant is starting to think. You've thought about it a little bit as well. I'm sure you've heard and agreed with the idea that you and your child should consider carefully where they want to live and who they want to live with and if they want to be rural or urban, enclosed campus or city campus, north or south, west or east. You might be forming so many ideas about safety schools, reach schools, and target schools. You might have strong opinions about the affordability of public and private, close to home and far away. Maybe you have ideas based on your own experience in school. Maybe your partner has an idea. Your uncle. Maybe your kid loves the color blue. A blue school would be nice.

Write all those schools down on your school list. A blue school. An appropriate school. A weird school. A fancy school. Write down schools that seem perfectly matched to your child based on the school write-ups and put little stars next to them. List schools that seem a little out there and a little wrong, but maybe? Write down schools that you certainly won't be able to afford (put money signs next to them) and ones that you've seen on a list of "most affordable" colleges. There are so many lists throughout the world. Google "best blue schools." These arbitrary categories offer helpful starting points for exploration.

I often hear parents say that they'd like their child to wait for college or maybe go to community college for a few years because their young person still has no idea what they want to do with their life. Prudently and sometimes a bit anxiously, parents explain that it would cost too much money to meander into a future. But meandering is vital when one walks into new. It is exploration. So don't be too afraid to meander into a four-year college on these lists. Put a community college down, too. Assemble the options.

Then, a little later, select the most affordable option that meets your family's needs. This exploration provides growth, even if you decide on a path that doesn't demand this work.

Make a Spreadsheet with Dates

Again, your applicant might not want you close to this process, but it is helpful for you to know when that first application is due so that you can appropriately back yourself off or step up to a last-minute panic. Respectful and diligent last-minute panics can be quite efficient.

There are some phrases that you need to know as you figure out dates. These phrases will have different meanings, contingencies, and deadlines for different schools so read the small print on the schools' websites.

As a side note, these categories can feel so confusing. Understanding them is kind of like understanding a super complicated board game. At first, you are absolutely lost and have to ask tons of questions and watch videos and make little maps for yourself. But then, once you get the logic, you can just roll. Hang in there and trust that you'll get it when it matters. Here's a start.

Rolling Admission

Colleges with rolling admission are probably already accepting applications. You can submit at these schools as early as July and all the way into April. Often, the earlier you apply, the better chance you have at money for these schools. If you have a rolling admission option that seems cool, suggest that your student apply early! An early application forces them to get first-draft material together. Also, these schools tend to have higher acceptance rates. You can keep one potential application or acceptance in your back pocket to start the process moving and, potentially, calm the fears of "I won't get in anywhere!"

Early Decision

Applying "early decision" means that you pick one and only one school that has an early decision option. You commit to going to that school if you get in. Therefore, you can't apply to more than one early decision school because, if you got in to more than one school early decision, you would have a conflict. You would be obligated to go to both of those schools, which would be impossible. You pick your one early decision school, you apply, you get in, you are done with applications, and then you go there. Or you pick one, you apply, you don't get in, and you know. Then, you apply to other schools. The early decision option tends to give students a better chance (sometimes a much better chance) at admission, but it takes away their opportunity to consider other colleges and financial packages.

Early decision allows schools to profit from the increased odds at higher payers because those who apply early decision often have the funds to gamble a bit with financial packages. So, an early decision school can find highly qualified, high-paying people to fill their spots early.

Early decision also allows schools to grab great students before they commit to other places. Let's say Duke wants to get a bunch of Olympians and International Science Fair winners. Those Olympians and science fair winners might be unsure of their chances at schools slightly higher up the ranking system—Harvard, say. The Olympians and science fair winners might think they have a better chance of getting into Duke early decision than they would of getting into Duke regular decision or Harvard any decision. So, they go for Duke early decision to up their odds at a favorite place. Duke, then, wins this student who might have chosen Harvard if they played the months out. A little weird, but the logic seems to work for many of those involved. It doesn't work great for students with less money who can't gamble like that.

People ask if they can legally back out of an acceptance from early decision if the financial package is bad. The answer is maybe, maybe not, probably with some ethically questionable behavior that might involve lawyers, but it really isn't cool.

Early Action

If you apply early action, you are taking advantage of an early deadline that *might* give you a better shot at admission, financial aid, and scholarship money. You are not bound to go to the school, though. Many colleges automatically enter early action students for scholarships. For some of these schools, early action applications are the *only* ones that are considered for scholarships. It makes sense to apply early action to large public schools if at all possible. Large public schools include state flagship colleges like the University of Maryland, the University of Michigan, and the University of Oregon—schools with state names in them. To all rules, however, there are exceptions. For example, California state schools don't often have early action or early decision, though some have priority admissions. Reading the fine print is important.

Restrictive Early Action

This is a form of early action in which you *cannot* apply early decision or restrictive early action to other private schools in a similar category, though you may apply early action to other public schools. For example, you can apply restrictive early action to Harvard, but then you *cannot* apply restrictive early action to Yale, Princeton, or Stanford. Further, if you apply restrictive early action to Harvard, you *cannot* apply early decision to schools that offer early decision, like Duke, per our previous example. Though, importantly, you can still apply early action to the University of Illinois and other state schools—and you should.

Only a few elite schools use this option. Applying restrictive early action may give you a very slight advantage because the acceptance rate is often a bit higher during the early action round, though you might be competing against higher-caliber students, making your advantage negligible. Notably, you don't have to gamble with financial packages with restrictive early action. You are free to choose your favorite school later on, after all of your acceptances have come in, without any binding obligations.

If your application is perfect and if you are aiming at very selective schools, you should pick one to apply restrictive early action. Then, you should also apply early action to all of your favorite public schools. And you should apply regular action to all of the other private schools. Restrictive early action lets a student declare that they like Princeton more than Harvard or that they prefer Georgetown over Yale, but they don't have to act on these preferences. In these highly competitive arenas, it might matter a tiny bit, and that tiny bit might be significant. But if you apply early with a less-than-polished application, you might be doing yourself a disservice.

Drop Those Colleges onto a Map

Are any of the locations close enough that you might pop up, down, or over this weekend or next weekend? Are you spontaneous enough to schedule a quick road trip? Or buy a cheap flight?! I bet you can roundtrip somewhere for $62 (if you commit to no carry-ons)—your baby and you on a trip, away from stress, absorbing the last of this stage!?

Now that you have the first major emotional hurdle of the rough draft out of your way and the roughest of college lists sketched, it's the perfect time to check out a school. Any school. It doesn't even have to be one that you love. Until you walk on a campus, look through some windows, and smell the history of a hallway, you can't really trigger the excitement for applying to college. Once your kid sees how happy and interesting and fun these spaces are, they tend to find enthusiasm and then the whole process is a bit easier. Schedule a tour on the college website if you can find availability. No worries if you can't. Just go.

As a family, have so much fun. Fall in love with every place you visit (unless you absolutely can't, then you know to leave it and other schools like it off your list). Yelp the best coffee shops and splurge on expensive drinks. Eat college foods (tacos, ramen, açaí, pizza) at a college restaurant (mismatched chairs) with college people (stickered laptops lighting adorable, eager faces). Bring frisbees to use green spaces. Arrive early to run on running trails. Pull on handles and walk through hallways. Slide into lecture halls. Marvel at libraries. Be aware of the size, the setup, and the structure of the buildings. Take pictures. Those pictures will be helpful to your student as they reconstruct why they love the university for supplemental essays and big decisions.

If you can't afford the time or money to visit right now, sit with your child as you watch YouTube. "Day in the life" videos are a thing. Sweet students walk you around campuses. Helpful and lovely. Just search "day in the life [your college's name]" or "student life [your college's name]" or "college tour [your college's name]."

Picture Your Student and Yourself in All Those Places

There are so many places and ways to be happy. There are endless opportunities for growth and learning. You and your child will feel much better about things once you realize the bounty. Abundance is comforting.

Tell Two People about Your Week 3 Life Betterment Plan

As you move into the realm of abundance, into the idea that you can be anything and do anything, let your life open up. Dang, as we age, it's so easy to close up the dream shop and settle down into some good old senescence. But we don't need to die yet, in any way. Open up your eyes to everything that is still available to you—new languages, trips, occupations, instruments, emotional depth, inner peace, relationships—and force yourself to consider the possibilities by telling other people about your pursuits. Sharing your plan or your wisp of a plan puts you on the line for carrying it out. This will make you a bit vulnerable. It's important and good practice to be vulnerable to the possibility of failure, success, or change. This feeling will also help you empathize with your college person.

Week 5, September 20–26

AM I QUIRKY ENOUGH?

You know that the pervasive insistence on quirk in college applications is a real fascination of mine. The college people used to like "well-rounded," which has gone out of fashion. I've also heard "spikey"—you should be great at a lot of things but world-changing in one or two spike areas. But "quirky," as the present characteristic of choice, is growing on me. I think I know how and why the college people made this word so important. At the last colleges meeting, when the colleges gathered to talk about what colleges do, they decided they want you to be quirky. When they ask you to be quirky, they are asking you to be authentic, but not boringly authentic. They want the most unique parts of you, but those should be packaged in the everyday. They don't necessarily want the video game part of you, but they would love to understand the video game part of you that makes you different from all the other video game kids. They want you to dig deep into your video game habits, motivations, and idiosyncrasies until you find something on the cusp of your consciousness that descends down into your childhood, your basest fears, and your most heroic possibilities. They want you to extricate your most magnificent and heartbreaking self from *Super Mario Bros* or *Fortnite* and hand it to them with poetry. Eighteen-year-old poetry. With youthful language. Casual. But tries really, really hard. This is their way of getting you to form a thesis or main argument for your college essay. It's pretty effective. They want you to isolate the center of your fabulousness from the life you have lived. Your fabulousness is there; I promise.

You are quirky enough! You are gorgeous, sensible, ridiculous, scrupulous, proud, unconventional, boisterous, responsible, and extravagant! You are so many things, and you haven't even begun to consider them yet. It's okay. You're young! You have been busy doing your homework. You've also been trying to navigate this almost-adult world, which can be socially, emotionally, academically, and economically chall-eng-ing!

You're quirky enough, too, grown adult person. You are capable, valuable, resilient, and ready.

This week, we are going to consider your most fabulous characteristics as we construct a second draft. Your characteristics are already present in your atrocious essay and your lists—your favorite things, the things that have happened to you, and the things that are important. We just have to identify these characteristics and mark them with words. I asked AI to give me a list of five hundred nonrepeating positive characteristic words. *Resilient* appeared on the list four times. *Quirky* didn't make it at all. I messed with the AI machine for a very long time and kept getting weird repeats and strange absences. I ended up with a gazillion wonderful words (AI can be amazing!) after using my own head to painstakingly remove and add for hours and hours (AI can be problematic!). Human brains are amazing and also problematic, which makes them quite quirky and useful for this project! I'll share my AI/human-generated word list with you later in the chapter when we will set to work on isolating your quirk.

But first, a note on AI: Don't use it to write your essays. At its best, AI will get in your way. AI considers all the people and ideas out there and jams them together into an amalgamation of thought from which it extracts the most probable arrangement of words to meet your needs. It's a cool and potentially helpful tool for so many things but *not* for your college essays. AI tends toward the formulaic, cliché, and impersonal. You want the opposite. You want to create something outside of the amalgam. You want to be unlikely. Likeably unlikely. Quirky. So, AI doesn't work for this project.

Also, if you use AI to construct your essay, you probably will be detected and potentially disqualified from admission. Your readers will sense the AI and feel sad. I know I sense it when I read its constructions. Then I run the material I sense through an AI checker. I am always right, by way of the checker machine software, which isn't always right. That software is not perfect and even has its own biases; however, it does give confidence to hunches, and then, your admissions officers might reluctantly pass you by.

But more critically, you don't need it! You can do this so much better than the machine. Don't use AI for your essays.

STUDENTS

Lovingly Consider Your Rough Draft Material

Your rough draft and your lists provide materials for your essay project. It helps to think about this material like you might think about the materials you use in the first stages of a building project or a cooking project. If you are building a house, you first need to gather up a bunch of wood and nails and cement. If you are making a cake, you have to bring many ingredients from the cupboard and your cabinets over to your counter. Some of the materials might be fabulous (a piece of marble, a perfect little brown egg, an authentic sentence), and some are potentially useful at best (bolts, flour, an explanation). When configured lovingly, these materials can create beautiful things, but the configuration is critical.

As you consider your rough draft, you may just want to start over, to metaphorically burn down that first humble structure of your house or to clear your counter with a swoop of your arm that cracks eggs on the floor and spreads flour across the countertop.

You may feel angry that you haven't already created brilliance. Be gentle with your eggs and flour and your two-by-fours and nails—the materials of your thought. They just need a little mixing, sawing, rearranging, and amending.

Assemble your writing, maybe printed out or open-tabbed—the lists, the paragraphs, the ideas.

Begin Working with That Rough Draft Material

Read your atrocious rough draft. Underline or highlight your favorite parts—at least three. Why do you like those parts? Is your writing particularly beautiful or just right in some phrases or sentences? Does it feel authentic and true? Does a memory feel strong and emotional? Great!

Reread your lists. Star or highlight the items that feel important, pretty, or evocative but that didn't make it into your first draft.

If you feel a little lost, hating your rough draft and yourself, feeling totally despondent, take a breath. Everyone—*everyone*—feels like this from time to time. Did you have one great idea that died an immediate death? Again, no worries. It is very hard to bring a brand-new thought into the world. You are jumping from something given—an event, a thing, an idea—to something potentially quite complicated at your core, in your past, in your dreams for the future.

Here are three steps you might take to move forward or inward, regardless of your current confidence in your work:

Expand Your Writing

Take any of your favorite parts or central parts and write more for five minutes. You might do three or four sets of this five-minute activity, corresponding to your favorite little chunks of rough draft material. Set a clock to force yourself to move, and then keep going if you're on a roll. Write long! You can cut later. Cutting, my friends, is no problem. Exceed word limits! Your brain needs the space to work things out.

If your writing is somewhat vague or idea based, write out a story or moment in detail that exemplifies or pinpoints the vagueness of the idea. If you already have a lovely story or an image, add more detail by including sensory descriptions—sights, sounds, smells, tastes, feels. Or add a parallel story or image (from your lists maybe). The conjunction of two stories might illuminate a cool thing about your preferences or thinking patterns.

An Example of Expansion

I had this one student who had so much to share, so many stories, so many accomplishments. As a result, it was hard for him to get into the details of any one thing. His draft started a little like a resume. Here is his rough draft introduction:

> **Rough Draft Start:** *I have been a part of many groups and organizations throughout my life, including the Boy Scouts of America, Soccer, Karate, Track, Cross Country, and many other school clubs. Out of every program and organization I have been a part of, the Boy Scouts of America has had the largest impact on me, turning me into the person I am today.*

Though his accomplishments are impressive, they aren't super exciting to read until they are expanded. To make matters worse, the people on the admissions committee are inundated with lists. They must read them in essays, again in the extracurricular section of the application, and in resumes if they request them. They certainly get tired of resume-like writing. To make a compelling essay, this student needed to pick one story to start with, to show the particular way in which the Boy Scouts have challenged him. In the following excerpt, you can see how he revised his start. Forgotten brick anchors can be more fabulous than Eagle Scout badges.

> **Revised Start:** *On the day of my Eagle Project, I thought I was prepared. I had checked and double-checked my plan and materials, but one aspect slipped through the cracks: the brick anchors for my display case were wrong.*

> With this new start, we can see so much more about this person! He is not only careful, ambitious, and responsible but also humble. We could see some of his ambition in the first start, but not much more. And we want to know what happens now! We want to read on. How does he get himself out of this conflict? Will he get the right brick anchors in time?!

Question Yourself

You can also expand your rough draft by asking yourself questions. So many questions! Take an idea or story from your essay and poke at it for a bit. For example, if you argue, "fear motivates me to be my best person," question yourself as you write. Why? How? Is the opposite true? Does security also motivate me? Or in some ways, does fear hinder me? Does fear work the same way on all people? Am I special? Does my privilege allow me to feel safe? Does my lack of security make me comfortable with fear? Might fear work differently on those who have faced scarier circumstances? How would this type of fear I describe play through the life of someone who is quieter, smaller, or of a different gender orientation, race, or religion? How would this idea feel to someone who lives in Paris, Quito, Kyoto, or Kolkata? As you answer these questions, your thinking will become more interesting. You can literally ask some of these same questions about anything you write!

So whatever you say, ask: Why? How? Does this work for everyone? Is the opposite of what I am saying also true? What makes my idea work for me in a way that it doesn't for other people?

An Example of Enriching Your Writing through Questions That Poke at a Premise or Central Idea

I told you about my lovely student who was hesitant to write about the death of her friend. Instead, she wanted to write about an idea surrounding the incident. She noticed that life tends to present itself with an equal balance of good and bad. You can see her rough draft with this idea in "Essay 4, First Rough Draft," page 190.

In the practice of expanding her rough draft, she questioned the idea that life presents itself in balance. She wondered, *Does it really? Do people in war-torn countries feel this balance? Do people who have recently lost a child feel this balance?* She recognized that her premise, while true in some situations and ways of looking, was absolutely untrue in other ways. Life can be a bit unfair to some. Many people must call on greater resilience to deal with unequitable conditions. Her luck, she acknowledged, made her "good" much easier to access and her "bad" much easier to manage. This thought offered her a jump in her thinking. She changed her essay and even changed her idea about what she wanted to do with her life. It was such an exciting development. To see how her idea transformed, check out "Essay 4, First Rough Draft," page 190, and "Essay 4, Final," page 191. Within these examples, you can see how she expanded like crazy—infusing her stories with beautiful sensory images. You can also see how she includes some listy details from her life (lists that show your fabulousness aren't all bad!), but they happen way later in her essay as a way to give evidence for what she's saying, not as an introduction.

An Example of Enriching Your Writing through Questions That Poke at Your Inner Self

Another student wrote a delightful little paragraph about how much she likes to explore the woods. I asked her why this exploration is so important to her. She struggled for a bit with the question. She also likes to feel the connections of cities. I asked her why. That question was tricky, too. The problem wasn't that she couldn't think about this stuff (she is quite a capable thinker), but that she didn't want to and she didn't want to think about it with me quite yet. This revelation turned her essay into an amazing and interesting exploration of self. You can see this transformation in "Essay 5, First Rough Draft," page 193, and then "Essay 5, Final," page 194. She shares her inner world with us, without sharing more than is comfortable. It feels like an honor to read her work.

Clarify the Material in Your Rough Draft

If you took my instructions on rough draft writing to heart, you wrote as thoughts came to you, exploring stories quickly and in succession. You may have ended up with a jumble of ideas, not sure how they link. This jumble of material can be super productive to work with. Your task in this revision stage is to figure out how the elements of your jumble link. Clarify the linkages.

Maybe the linkages are obvious. You wrote about your dog's floppy ears, and then a time when your dog was sick, and then a time when you were sick, and your favorite soup. Is there something about comfort that is interesting to you? Write a comfort sentence next to each snippet. Then, throw questions at this comfort idea until you come up with an interesting central question and answer. Am I a comfortable person? Am I the opposite of comfortable? What do I like and hate about being uncomfortable?

Or your snippets might be utterly unrelated. You might have written about frozen Snickers bars, then something that happened in French class, then your favorite fashion blog. Play a game with yourself and see if you can find any common element. You might write a fictive story about your future self, eating a caramel nut crème brûlée (is this a thing?) in a French café as passersby comment on your Chanel suit. Maybe you are a Taurus and, as such, are enthralled with sensuous experiences—candy, cashmere, Parisian culture. It doesn't matter as long as you can find a through line that screams out your loveliness. Then, use that through line to attach all the cool stories that are central to your experience as a human.

An Example on How to Clarify Linkages

One student took the advice to draft through tiny details so well, there were a million beautiful little snippets all smashed together. You can see this cool draft on page 196, "Essay 6, First Rough Draft." He didn't worry about punctuation or perfection. He just wrote things that are important to him, and it worked out great.

As he moved toward his first set of revisions, he needed to clarify the linkages of all his beautiful snippets. He didn't necessarily need to add more, until he figured out why the ideas he explored came together as they did. He was clearly writing about culture, family, and sleep. He needed to figure out the link between those three things. In the end, he recognized the time difference between the locations of the two major sections of his family served him, and he used this unifying strand to make something incredibly creative. Read his final ("Essay 6, Final") on page 199.

Search for Your Thesis

Knowing what a thesis is can change your view of learning in quite an exciting way. In academia (the world of colleges and universities), a thesis is often described as an argument. These "arguments," however, aren't just forceful and conflictive things one must swallow to learn. They are nuanced attempts to create something new for the world. When you go to college, you will gradually become a thesis machine. With your theses, you will create knowledge where there isn't knowledge. It's not just about learning anymore, my dears! It's about creating! You will create many new things for the world!

Your education thus far might have revolved around learning what is given to you—memorizing the notes from your teachers' lectures or from your textbooks. Your teachers tell you something, a book offers you a lesson or a story, and you internalize those stories and lessons to show you have *gained* knowledge. But college, at its most exciting and effective, is about *producing* knowledge. You learn what there is to learn, and then you figure out the unexplored spaces within that learning. You poke questions at the thing you know. You rethink. You wonder! Your essay (and all your work going forward in life) should be filled with this wonder and your attempts to consider the wonder's reason for being.

You won't just make theses in class. You will stay up late in dining halls or sprawl lazily on lawns and have serious debates about the nature of being, the structure of political systems, the depth and dangers of algorithmic utility. You may argue back and forth with teachers and other students, stretching your thought and sharpening your communication. Argument making and in particular, thesis writing, can be an ambitious form of shaping the new, shaping your brain, shaping the world. But theses can also be softer and humbler revelations. Your essay and your process of thesis creation can take on many forms from bombastic claims to quiet perceptions. Regardless, I hope you become a producer of knowledge in this most delicious of ways. And in these applications, I hope you create something new for yourself, for your favorite college, and for the world. Growth, vision, hope!

Write Your Thesis

Considering your essay, your thesis should focus on the wonder and the puzzle of you. Who are you? What makes you unique? How does your mind work? What pulls at your thoughts? What is in your heart? Your answer to these questions will create your thesis—something new and wonderful you come to as you draft.

Your thesis tells your reader what you are teaching them about you. It might fit right after your first story or later in your draft. You probably won't know what it is until you are almost done writing but keep wondering about it. Keep asking yourself, *What am I saying about myself that is new?*

Here are some examples from the essays in the addendum.

Essay 1

The prototyping I learned at the sewing machine gives me the freedom to create things tailored exactly to my vision. . . . I want to build a life where I can bridge the design thinking, prototyping, and building that I love with a real understanding of what the world needs.

This author's thesis comes at the end in two sections. I don't know that she was even aware that she had a thesis. A good thesis can show up after you've done good thinking that structurally gels. The author kind of worked her way toward her thesis and, with it, clarified everything that had come before. In your essays, this can work well because you want your reader to get transported right to your central point. In academic essays that you write for your classes, you will plant your thesis in the first couple of paragraphs so people know what you are doing. In any case, when you are creating a thesis, you probably won't figure it out clearly until you are done drafting. The writing provides the thinking you need to figure out what you are saying.

Essay 2
I pursue openings of unknowns where my brain belongs. I methodically and joyfully find my place in the expanse of time and space.

This author also comes to her thesis in the end. You can see the little side points along the way that build up to her central idea.

> Side point A: *With math as my justification and power, I found belonging in space.*

> Side point B: *If multiplying Seager variables shows me where I belong in space, then picking up a Galápagos tortoise shows me where I belong in time.*

> Side point C: *I find belonging by negotiating cultural under-standing. . . . Belonging is this responsibility to lead, but it's also a responsibility to listen, follow, and learn.*

Essay 3
My ability to hyper fixate on how things affect people, my encyclopedic knowledge of geography and history, and some serious math skills have led to my college interest in Geography, GIS, and Cartography.

Essay 4
[The world's problems and injustices] are massive systemic issues that cannot be easily fixed, but I want to take my next step in making change with a double major in psychology and public policy—one to learn about introspective changes we can make as individuals, and the other to learn what we can do for our society.

Essay 5
To truly connect, regardless of physical and emotional proximity, we must understand each other and learn to look at the world from a new perspective.

Essay 6
Sleep isn't just rest; it's what connects me to my roots, my family, and my identity. It lets me feel truly at home no matter where I am.

Guidelines for the Theses of Your Life

- Your answer shouldn't be too general. *I am a person who cares about others*, for example, is too obvious. We are all this kind of person, to some extent. There's no point in saying something that many people might be able to say. *I love to learn. The trials in my life have made me stronger. People are good. Poetry makes me happy. I like science because I am good at it.* If you can find a dozen people in your class who could argue the same thing, push yourself deeper by asking questions. Why? How? Does this work for everyone? Is the opposite of what I am saying also true? What makes my idea work for me in a way that it doesn't for other people?
- Your thesis must be plausible in its specificity; it shouldn't be so ridiculous that you can't back it up. Now, you might call yourself a superhero, which could be implausible, but if you back it up with funny data that shows the ways in which this is true, great! Evidence is crucial for plausibility. If you don't have good stories or data to offer as evidence to your thesis, your reader will have no reason to believe what you say.
- Your thesis should be interesting and important to your audience. You can tell your admissions person about your dog or your grandma, but unless your stories link back to you and your unique characteristics, your reader probably won't be that interested.

> - Your thesis should be clear and concise. It might cover a couple of sentences, or you might use some commas and semicolons to keep it together.

So what's the thesis for your rough draft? Write it down. This will be a struggle—because your rough draft is atrocious, remember? You are just starting to expand, question, and arrange materials. So write down a thesis for what you think you might be trying to say. Does it stay within the guidelines listed here? If not, make it more specific, more plausible, more interesting, and clearer. Then, keep writing!

Your new thesis will be the kernel around which you write your next draft. Then, you will change and amend your thesis again, all the way to the very end of your process. Your thesis will continue to change as you figure out what you're talking about. *This* is the process of good writing and good thinking; you will dance from one thesis to the next as you dig deeper and think harder.

Identify Your Most Charming Characteristics

In this section, you will find a list of characteristics that might help you structure your essay. Pick out the words that resonate with you. Do they relate to your behavior in your stories? These words can help you identify why your stories are important. Once you pick your words, place them in your essay in multiple forms, several times, with examples. You can tell your readers directly that you are enthusiastic. You might tell your readers that you brush your teeth enthusiastically. Or you might say that you could be mistaken for a golden retriever in a tennis ball factory. Once you identify who you are, make sure you are clearly giving that specific description of you to your reader. A great essay should give your reader at least three fundamental traits that define you. What do your stories say about who you are?

AM I QUIRKY ENOUGH?

Are You . . .?

Kind Brave Compassionate Generous Resilient Empathetic Honest Courageous Optimistic Loyal Patient Wise Creative Humble Reliable Curious Passionate Authentic Assertive Supportive Determined Grateful Joyful Forgiving Open-Minded Confident Adaptable Selfless Resourceful Respectful Enthusiastic Caring Thoughtful Cheerful Ambitious Tolerant Understanding Flexible Resolute Tenacious Modest Serene Balanced Reflective Empowered Versatile Industrious Enterprising Unwavering Sympathetic Charismatic Persuasive Astute Invigorated Vibrant Grounded Focused Innovative Imaginative Intuitive Persistent Disciplined Altruistic Magnanimous Gallant Amiable Genuine Kindhearted Benevolent Heartwarming Self-Assured Reassuring Spirited Fervent Unstoppable Relentless Dynamic Energetic Robust Lively Buoyant Bubbly Invincible Chaste Dominant Dramatic Dreamy Articulate Autonomous Aware Beautiful Approachable Sociable Gregarious Outgoing Extroverted Warm Sincere Open Transparent Direct Frank Candid Unassuming Down-to-Earth Soft-Hearted Loving Nurturing Sensitive Gentle Polite Courteous Well-Mannered Considerate Civil Sophisticated Refined Gracious Chivalrous Urbane Dignified Elegant Poised Stylish Fashionable Encouraging Uplifting Inspirational Motivational Reassuring Comforting Consoling Soothing Empowering Affirming Appreciative Positive Hopeful Radiant Enchanting Jubilant Magnetic Captivating Vivacious Exuberant Charming Fascinating Intriguing Eloquent Diplomatic Polished Suave Graceful Classy Distinguished Noble Majestic Regal Magnificent Splendid Glorious Resplendent Illustrious Exquisite Grand Opulent Sumptuous Luxurious Statuesque Praiseworthy Tactful Witty Humorous Amusing Entertaining Hilarious Playful Quirky Lighthearted Droll Cheeky Zany Eccentric Offbeat Comical Chucklesome Gleeful Merry Frolicsome Rollicking Riotous Side-Splitting Belly-Laughing Rib-Tickling Hysterical Laughable Goofy Silly Absurd Ridiculous Farcical Satirical Parodic Jocular Fun-Loving Jesting Giggle-Inducing Unconventional Whimsical Idiosyncratic Unorthodox Singular Oddball Unusual Peculiar Quizzical Unpredictable Anomalous Outlandish Novel Nonconformist Freakish Curious Aberrant Funny

Chunk Up Your Essay

Okay, I've asked you to pick some characteristics to throw about, add sensorial details to your stories, dig into your main arguments producing depth, and write a thesis that is complex and plausible. How do you shape these things into an essay? How will you structure your complex and adorable life into a package that will be clear, scintillating, entirely unique, and perfectly authentic?

You probably know the classic five-paragraph essay that is often taught in high school: Tell them three things you plan to tell them, tell them those things with evidence, and then conclude, reminding them what you told them. This structure is solid. It solves one of the greatest difficulties in writing. Your reader is kind of dumb. I mean, they're not dumb about all things, but they are a bit lost when it comes to the complex inner workings of your brain. You're probably still somewhat lost when it comes to the complex inner workings of your brain. Structure helps you organize your ideas so that you can figure out what you're trying to say while helping your reader move through their tragic inability to follow the delightful weirdness of you.

But it is a wonderful thing to outgrow the five-paragraph structure. You may have felt your ideas oozing out of the paragraph cracks and bursting through the conclusion seams for some time now. This is as it should be. Five paragraphs don't give space for critical asides, opposite viewpoints, or funny extensions. As your ideas have grown more complex, you might have found yourself writing very long five-paragraph-essay body paragraphs. Those get hard to read. You're going to want to give your essay readers zippy little paragraphs that punch the bits of you into their flesh.

Feel free to ditch the idea of five paragraphs, but grab at two or three or four chunks (which can consist of multiple paragraphs each). You can chunk things in any way you want. You might say one thing, then the opposite, then move on to a related idea: I'm afraid of everything; I'm not afraid of anything; I want to study cancer, which makes me afraid and not afraid.

You might chunk things in terms of your stories: I swallowed a worm when I was seven. I refused to dissect worms when I was fifteen. Look at how funny and morally righteous and prepared for anatomy I am!

You might want to deliver the hard part of a story, then a relevant intellectual opinion, then the joyful conclusion to your story.

You might chunk up your stories based on your personal characteristics. The way you eat spaghetti shows you're (a) inclusive, (b) creative, and (c) humble. Then wrap things up with a thesis statement and maybe a look toward the future. More on this in a minute.

The chunks will help you manage the flow of your brain. They'll also help your reader follow you and feel your narrative.

It is a wonderful thing to step away from your work and have a conversation with yourself (while you're running, showering, falling asleep, waiting for a bus, waiting for a teacher). What am I doing with this essay, and what are some chunks that can help me get through it?

Consider Ending with a Chunk about Your Future

Relate your thesis, your stories, and your personal characteristics to your college plans. Your essay might actually help you figure out what you want to do!

Remember how I told you what happened with the "even balance of good and bad" person? Originally, she thought it would be cool to help people see the even balance in their lives through therapy, but she decided that it wouldn't address the problems of social inequity. She decided to shift her course of study so she might eventually become a lawyer, to create more just systems. So exciting, my friends!

Let your stories, your personal characteristics, and the pieces of your argument lead you freely into the conclusion of your essay and into your future. Again, don't worry yet about which particular essay prompt you choose! Your essay will lead you to the prompt. If it doesn't, one of the prompts is a write-about-anything prompt. That'll work.

CONCERNED ADULTS
Help Your Student with Their Essay

This week, your person is working on their essay. Hopefully, they will want you to check it out soon. These are the elements you should look for:

- Stories from their life! The best way for them to show who they are is to replay little essential clips from their life. These clips might be as simple as walks with a dog, adventures at Dunkin' Donuts, or getting gas for the first time. Don't worry if the stories aren't the biggest moments. The little moments tend to be more unique.

    You may be tempted to push your person to include all of their major accomplishments in this essay. No need to squeeze these lists in (awards, GPA, extracurricular achievements) because there will be other spaces for their accomplishments throughout the application.

- You should be able to feel their stories through sensory details: colors, shapes, sounds, smells, textures, flavors, and such.

- The essays should make clear your person's proudest and most prominent characteristics: check out the characteristics list in the "Are You . . . ?" textbox on page 79. Does the essay clearly demonstrate who they are? If they are effervescent, does that word make it into the essay? If not effervescent, how about *bubbly, charismatic, frenetically adorable*? Which personality traits are evident in their essays? Help them see those wonderful personal attributes that they embody and show them how to adjective, verb, and noun with those words throughout their writing.

- The essay should carry their voice. If your person is funny, humor is fantastic. If they are feisty and enthusiastic, scrappy language is totally appropriate. They will be at their most respectful when they are their most authentic. I promise you that they do not need to use serious and formal style in this essay (unless they are serious and formal people, then by all means). They shouldn't be crude or disrespectful, but as long as they are nice, they should feel free to write like they talk.
- The essay should be clear. If you're not sure where the essay is going, you might help by writing a sentence next to each paragraph that shows what you *think* they are trying to say. Asking questions is helpful.
- At the drafting stage in writing, many writers need to rearrange. Paragraphs and sentences can be shuffled to make better meaning, like a deck of cards can be shuffled to make a better hand. You might hold all the spades, hearts, clubs, and diamonds in order. You could put your aces on one side of your hand and the twos on the other. Offer suggestions if you have an organizational idea and your student is open to hearing it.
- Their essays should be absolutely free of errors, but it might be a little too early in the game to help them make things too shiny. They might still need to shuffle ideas around.
- Soon, they'll need to cut words, but not yet. If something doesn't make sense, they should add, add, add, add! Give your student the confidence to write more! You never know when the most gorgeous sentence might fall. The more sentences they write, the better the odds are that they hit on great beauty. Help them not worry about word limits.

- As you go through this essay, your person might be scared that you hate it. Maybe you hate it? I hope not. But it's possible. Sometimes essays can be quite a mess before they are wonderful. But at this point, and really every point, more than anything else, it is your job to tell your person what you love. You can follow up if you'd like, and if there is an opening, to suggest edits. But mostly, give love.

Don't Help Your Student with Their Essay

This line of nonengagement might be better. Is your kid pulling their hair out? Feeling tremendously insecure as they put their life onto paper? This middle part of the process often feels like nothing will ever work. Your student might not be ready for you yet. They may need a minute.

Here are some things you might say to help them find that confidence:

- I see how hard you are working! My last years in high school weren't nearly as stressful. Or, my last years in high school were so stressful but in different ways.
- You doing okay? Can I make you bucatini/bulgogi/brisket?
- I am so proud of you! (Even if they are a mess, right? They are engaging, which is kind of a big deal.)
- I'm here to help you whenever you need me. I know how hard writing can be!

Help Your Student Identify Their Most Salient Characteristics While You Identify Your Own

Dears, being a parent is wildly wonderful and immensely tricky. We don't sleep enough, and we multitask everything. We clean and organize things that are intended to be dirtied and disorganized. We give, save, and invest without any evidence that our precious products will end up okay. We pour all of our love and attachment into little beings who will leave us if we are successful. It's a trip. And we get older by the day, as they do. It's easy to lose oneself in the shuffle.

But there is a full *you* inside of you! When your kids leave your house, you may have an opportunity to reacquaint the person you have become with that covered up stuff from an earlier era. But why not do it now? It will make their leaving easier. You have much of your identity yet to project and many important things yet to do. While you help your person figure out who they are, go ahead and give it a shot for yourself, too. Go through the characteristics list in the "Are You . . . ?" textbox on page 79 and pick some words out for yourself.

Gather Your Resources

Do you have a friend, neighbor, former teacher, grocer, bookstore clerk, or sister-in-law who writes, teaches writing, is decently interesting in emails, is good at grammar, is empathetic, went to a lot of school? It's a good time to connect your student with editing help. Your student needs a few sets of eyes on their essays. It is not cheating for your student to ask for help with grammar, to talk with others about clarity, to brainstorm ideas. It is cheating to have someone else write the essay. The line is clear.

When you do find wonderful helper people, you might send them a copy of this chapter or at least the tips from the first item in this section if you think they could use them or would appreciate a little guidance. Also, send them the tips from the second item in this section, so they remember that this writing is a vulnerable process that requires lots of kindness.

Even when you find the best helpers, they might not give the best advice. Your student can follow their gut, accepting what feels helpful and true and ignoring the rest.

Remind your student to thank these helpers with a nice letter or even a little gift—a candle or cup of coffee—once they finish the process.

Check on Recommendation Letters

This is just a reminder that you should remind your child to remind their teachers about their recommendation letters. There's an art to these check-ins; no one wants to nag or be nagged. Again, your student's letter writers are likely very busy and may be using the deadline to arrange their tasks. So they probably are on it, but you have to make sure. This letter should be from your student, not you. It's so good for them to practice these communications! And everyone wants to see their adultness emerge. Here is some language your student might try out:

Hi Ms. Letterwriter!

I wanted to thank you again for writing a letter for me. Thank you!

Also, I thought you might be interested in checking out the second draft of my essay. I am excited about the story around our family garden but still trying to figure out how to connect it to my future plans. I'd love any of your thoughts or comments on it, but please, don't feel obligated. I know you're so busy this time of the year.

Let me know if I can help you in any way as you write my letter and get it into the portal. I think I already gave you the deadline but in case this information is helpful, your recommendation letter should be emailed to Mr. Guidance Counselor by [date]/submitted into [x] portal by [date].

I hope you have a great week!

Really appreciate you,
Frog

Or something shorter:

Dear Mr. Letterwriter,
    I hope you had a great weekend! I am a person who loves reminders so I thought you might appreciate one. I just wanted to remind you that my recommendation letter is due [in this format on this date to this person].
    Again, thank you so much!

I am truly grateful,
Frog

Sketch a List of Your Student's Extracurriculars

I'm keeping you busy here, trying to keep you away from the danger zone of the essay. Look at the first due date. You might be thinking, "Oh my gosh, there are just four weeks left!" Remember those essays you used to write in two hours before a deadline. Remember how much panic can flush brilliance from a body. You and your student have so many hours yet. Be patient and keep parenting. You got this!

    Brainstorming a list of your student's extracurriculars will help you make sure they don't forget anything important. They might undervalue some of their activities as every-kid-does-this stuff. You have been around longer, and you know their unique situations and abilities. Help them see the importance of their work, their caretaking, their talents, and the interesting ways they use their time.

Research Your Money Opportunities and Challenges

College is stupid expensive. For everyone. But of course, the more money you have, the easier it is for you to deal with it. The less money, the harder it is to enable magical or reckless thinking—*we'll just see where this goes; the money will appear; it'll be worth it.* In the end, everyone has to navigate the economic decisions in different ways, so it's hard to find perfectly fitted advice; and as luck goes, good advice might not have good outcomes. But dive in. You can do this! Did you finish your FAFSA?

- Here are a couple of good books: *Who Gets In and Why: A Year Inside College Admissions* by Jeffrey J. Selingo. He divides colleges into two groups: "buyers" and "sellers." For middle-income people, these categories are crucial to understand as you seek an affordable school. Also helpful is *The Price You Pay for College: An Entirely New Road Map for the Biggest Financial Decision Your Family Will Ever Make* by Ron Lieber. This is a comprehensive guide to help you through your financial questions.
- There are many free Facebook groups with tons of super helpful, utterly unhelpful, brilliant, and irritating pieces of advice. Do a search and join a few. Seek the groups out, not for certain directives, but to feel the types of questions you might ask yourself and financial officers. Take everything that everyone says with a grain of salt.
- There are two types of aid that might help you lower costs. Merit aid is money that is distributed to students based on their grades and talents. This can come from the colleges themselves, outside businesses, nonprofits, religious groups, or any other scholarship-giving organization.

    Need-based aid helps students and families afford college. It is entirely based on your family's economic situation. When you fill out your FAFSA, you are giving your financial information to schools so that they can figure out how much you can afford. The need-based college, state, and federal grants will help you cover expenses.
- Some schools give lots of need-based aid and little or no merit aid. Ivy League schools, for example, can be immensely

affordable if you come from a low- or middle-income family. They generally have a lot of money and more amazing applicants than they can handle. Their financial aid is entirely about balancing affordability for those who they admit. As I've encouraged before, apply to these schools if your stats are stellar and your finances are not, or even if your finances are pretty good. They might be your most affordable option.

- Other schools give tons of merit aid and little to no need-based aid. They are hoping to attract students so they use their merit awards to draw talent across economic levels.
- Many colleges give a combination of need-based and merit aid. Once you are accepted, you will receive a financial package from your school that should detail the school's financial assistance.
- Whatever financial package you receive, consider negotiating for more! You can ask your school's financial aid office about the appeal process if you are not happy with your offer. You might be able to offer additional details or tax forms from a more recent period.
- When thinking about scholarships, apply local and niche. If you are an oboe player, look for oboe scholarships. If you raise and sell cows, look for scholarships that reward livestock sellers. Check out your town's Rotary Club. See if your religious group offers money. Consider the Distinguished Young Women program. Does your city have an organization dedicated to lifting up local students? There are so many organizations that want to celebrate you, and there are many under-applied-to scholarships.
- Here are some resources to find scholarships and other money opportunities. *The Ultimate Scholarship Book: Billions of Dollars in Scholarships, Grants and Prizes* by Gen Tanabe

and Kelly Tanabe is huge and overwhelming but neatly organized, if you can motivate. Additionally, online and through your school's guidance counselors, you can access many more economic opportunities. Here are just a few places to start: https://bigfuture.collegeboard.org; https://studentaid.gov; and https://scholarships360.org.

Week 6, September 27–October 3

GETTING THINGS JUST RIGHT

Recently, I helped my fifth-grader go through a list of 450 progressively more difficult words, designed to prepare him for the elementary school spelling bee. Spelling bees are a special kind of torture. You can study and study but you know that, at the last minute, your mind might say, "Hey, wait a minute, isn't it an *e*?" And then the doubt will utterly take you down.

I really want him to win and he wants to win, but we also know that winning is possibly the worst outcome. He would probably learn more through a gracious loss. Even a tormented, everyone-is-watching-me, snotty-nosed crying loss could teach him a lot about losing and teach me a lot about parenting. Winning may bring a smiley minute of photographed joy, but we would then look out and see all the faces of sad kids and parents, tripped up by an *e*, who almost hate us a little bit in that moment. To make matters worse, spell check makes the whole point of spelling skills questionable. And, if he does win, we will have to do this all over at the county spelling bee. But in order to play along in this little elementary school game, he still has to try to get 450 sets of letter sequences exactly right. His brain and his mouth and his entire nervous system must spit everything out perfectly in order to win.

The importance of this process, though, my friends, is not in the perfection and certainly not in the winning (though I hope you win a *lot* in everything and especially in your applications!). The importance is in the trying so hard to get things just right. It is in my son lying on the dirty kitchen floor at 7 a.m. with the fuzzy brown couch blanket (which is not supposed to leave the living room) twisted around his little body. As my eleven-year-old practices with me, he curses skillfully after every missed word. (I've always told my kids that I don't care if they use bad words, as long as they never use words to hurt anyone's feelings. He took this to heart. I have created a crass little human.) But he is the most beautiful thing in the world, working so hard with me to achieve little pieces of perfection. We remind ourselves that winning the bee is not the point. Living a good life with blankets and kitchen floors and word-readers who love you so very much—practicing failure again and again so you become exceptionally brave at trying hard things—this is the point.

Dear students and loving adults, you have arrived at your spelling bee. It is time to work so hard to achieve little pieces of perfection, which might work or might not. Regardless of outcomes, if you approach this perfectionistic project wholeheartedly and include the people you love, it will be lovely. I hope that you are exceptionally brave as you enlist help. I wish you so much resilience as you recognize your imperfections. And I wish you patience and strength as you summon the energy to get things just right.

Seeking "just right" and the help to get there is necessary in two different arenas. First, you will fill in the short answers for your application. Each blank requires a precise focus. As you move through the first few questions—*name, address, date of birth, gender, nationality, language proficiency*—I imagine you slowing down, considering each box and bubble, writing yourself as you are, asserting your gender, considering your city of birth, acknowledging the languages that have brought you understanding, considering your path through time. Maybe you started filling these blanks in when the application came out, flying through the first few pages, getting things done. If that's the case, revisit each blank this week. Look at your answers. Double-check them with a perfectionist's eye. Have someone else check, too—someone careful who loves you. Then press the Enter key. You've cemented that piece of your childhood. You've signed your perfect little answers to those simple questions that define you. You don't have to look back. That's it. This is you, for now.

Second, you will begin to perfect your lovely essay by asking for help. This can be terrifying, humbling, and gratifying. This is the lying-on-the-kitchen-floor-cursing process, which will get you absolutely everything in life. You will ask for help, those helpers will kindly point out problems, you will assess those problems, you will fix those problems, your essay will improve, and you will be smarter and braver. If you find yourself ready to give up, if you lean too hard into "I am done" before you should be done, they will say, "No, no, no, no, not yet, sweetie." And you will be angry but then you will work a little longer and you will be smarter and braver and your writing will be better. Equally, if you become too perfectionistic and self-thrashy, they will take your perfection by the hand, walk it to the door, and tell it to take a few breaths or go for a little walk. They can ensure that you keep your standards of "just right," even if you check out for a minute. Be so very proud of your hard work. Your capacity to get things just right is growing with every process like this. All this capacity-growing effort makes your life meaningful.

STUDENTS

Share Your Application Process

It is perfectly normal, at this point, to want to hide your application process from everyone. As you stumble through writing your life and nailing down your identity, it probably feels most comfortable to leave other people out of it. The extra doubt, concern, and criticism might be more than you can handle. And the college essay is among the most vulnerable of genres; you must expand upon your best qualities (what if other people don't believe in them?) and reveal your true self (do you have it right?). Wouldn't it be wonderful if you could just skip the sharing and head straight for the winning? The college of your dreams! Everyone will be so proud!

But you're going to be much less likely to get into that college of your dreams without some extra eyes on your essay. You can't skip the slightly embarrassing and potentially even heartbreaking acceptance of your imperfection. Now is the time to find your humility and just share. Be so proud of how humble you are, letting other people see your words, seeking to better yourself and your future prospects. Be proud that you aren't perfect yet because then that would be the end. You're not at the end.

Find someone who is good at grammar, someone who knows you well, and someone who loves to write. Pass out your essay to everyone and anyone. Grab at feedback from your teachers, counselors, relatives, and friends. The more feedback you receive, the better your essay will become and the better writer you will become.

Take Essay Feedback and Change Things (Or Don't)

If people aren't sure about a paragraph, ask them why. Can you shift your paragraph a little? Or maybe just get rid of it—put it in your "bad writing" document. Make space for something stunning. You can write a new paragraph in ten minutes! Don't be afraid of changes. Every time you write, you are likely to produce something better. All great writers rewrite and write new, again and again and again.

If a reader doesn't understand what you're trying to say in a sentence (or you don't understand what you're trying to say in a sentence), change it. Even if you love the creative flair or the pacing of a piece of writing, if it doesn't make sense, it's not worth it. Maybe you can keep the flair and enhance the clarity. As a rule, if one person doesn't understand exactly what you are trying to say, other people will struggle in similar ways. So just tweak it. If several of your people suggest the same problem, you should definitely make some changes. There are a million ways to say any one thing, so just pick one of the other million.

Beyond clarity issues, if you receive feedback that doesn't feel right, you can ignore it. Feedback isn't always right. Age and experience don't automatically make people better writers of your thoughts. Nor does strength of opinion. Your instincts might be spot-on while your teachers, parents, and friends are off. They don't know what it feels like to be you. They might be trying to make you more formal. This isn't a formal genre. If people try to make your essay sound smarter with bigger words, don't listen to them. Use the words that feel right to you.

Here are some simple guidelines that can help you rewrite. I'll show them to you with this great student sentence, full of marvelous detail, evocative images, and a clear look into her life. But I bet we can make it even better.

Example before Revision
Despite my borderline obsession with Taylor Swift, staying up till 3am with my dad to watch a rocket launch live stream is one of my favorite pastimes. We'd see it on the news the day of and make plans to watch whatever YouTube streamer we could find.

- Break a long or complicated sentence into two simpler sentences.
  Original: *Despite my borderline obsession with Taylor Swift, staying up till 3am with my dad to watch a rocket launch live stream is one of my favorite pastimes.*
  Revised: *I have a borderline obsession with Taylor Swift. But there is one thing that outshines Taylor: live-stream rocket launches.*

- Simplify the sentence structure: Subject, verb, object.
    Original: *We'd see it on the news the day of and make plans to watch whatever YouTube streamer we could find.*
    Revised: *My dad and I scour the news for upcoming launches.*
- Clarify pronouns like *this*, *it*, and *she*.
    Original: *We'd see it on the news the day of and make plans to watch whatever YouTube streamer we could find.*
    Revised: *We'd see the report of a 3 a.m. launch and make plans to watch whatever YouTube streamer we could find.*
- Make sure your tenses are as you would like them. If you can make something present tense and drop the conditionals, why not? Present tense can make writing a little more vibrant. Double-check that your tenses are consistent throughout your entire essay. It's perfectly fine to go from past to present, but make sure the past is consistently past tense and the present is consistently present tense. We'll shift the conditional in this example.
    Original: *We'd see it on the news the day of and make plans to watch whatever YouTube streamer we could find.*
    Revised: *We see the report of a 3 a.m. launch and make plans to watch whatever YouTube streamer we can find.*
- Put a sentence between two disjointed sentences to make the link clear. Or add a bunch of sentences! With this example, the writer could have talked about how these news reports look or the exact process of 3 a.m. watching. Do they stay up or wake up? Watch with snacks? Here, I don't think much is necessary because she has so many more details she covers in her essay, but the possibilities are really endless. She could add the word *when* to increase flow and add a few extra words to make the process come alive.
    Original: *We see the report of a 3am launch and make plans to watch whatever YouTube streamer we can find.*

Revised: *When we see the report of a 3 a.m. launch, we make plans to watch whatever YouTube streamer we can find. I wake my dad up, we make sandwiches, and sit in the dark at the kitchen table.*

- Take out extra words. If a word isn't serving a purpose, it is getting in the way. To get from the sentences above to this set, I actually added a few words. That's fine, if words give you greater clarity, as they often do. Words are easier to cut than you think, and they can always be cut from different sections. More on this in a bit!

Example after Revision

I have a borderline obsession with Taylor Swift. But there is one thing that outshines Taylor: live-stream rocket launches. My dad and I scour the news for upcoming launches. When we see the report of a 3 a.m. launch, we make plans to watch whatever YouTube streamer we can find. I wake my dad up, we make sandwiches, and sit in the dark at the kitchen table as a piece of earth leaves the atmosphere.

More Things to Consider

You might be asking yourself, *Should I really begin a sentence with "but" or "and"?* Are sentence fragments ever okay? Should I be using the word *I* in something as important as an admissions essay?

Yes. These stylistic choices are just fine, as long as you have mastered grammar and writing conventions. Now is the time in your life in which you can start to break conventions! If these moments of roguery have an effect. If you are breaking conventions for a reason. If they help your pacing, your clarity, or your poetic voice.

Now, if you are writing a formal essay for a humanities class—philosophy or English literature, maybe—stay within your conventions. You want your arguments to get the attention rather than the fancy writing with which you make them. Clarity is always key, especially when making complicated arguments.

If you are writing a social science paper, never use the passive voice. It obscures the important actors, the culpable parties, and the underrepresented voices. "Racism happened to slaves" is too forgiving. "White English colonizers enslaved Black people from African nations" gets more to the point and helps us untangle wrong things.

If you are writing a lab report, you will likely stay far away from the word *I*. It isn't important. Chemical compounds, biological structures, and mathematical equations become the stars. Passive voice helps them be the stars. Writing conventions have reasons for being. They become much more exciting once you understand why they exist and how they remake the world.

In this essay, which is about you and the way your brain works, you should definitely use *I*! You should definitely write the beauty and cadence of your thoughts, even if they break conventions.

Be Resilient as You Draft, Rearrange, and Change Your Essay
You might get to a point where you are so sick of what you are writing, you just can't. Suddenly, your essay might make zero sense. You might break down and cry or play *Brawl Stars* for three hours. When these moments hit, here's what you can do:

> **Ways to Become Unstuck**
>
> - Sit down with someone to talk about a paragraph. The presence of another person can force your brain to think.
> - Write sentences in the margins that describe what you are trying to do in each paragraph. These might bring clarity and might become actual topic sentences that help your reader make connections. If your new sentence makes absolutely no sense in the context of your essay, write one that does and then write the paragraph that goes with it.
> - Give yourself an assignment for one conceptual problem and work on it in a ten-minute meeting with yourself. Are

> you being totally honest and authentic in a paragraph? Is there a part of you that hasn't made it through yet? Does a paragraph feel forced? Are there disjointed sections? What would you need to say to be authentic, real, clear, and cohesive?
> - Read a memoir or some poetry and notice how other people pour their hearts into words.
> - Beside or above your existing paragraphs, write simple and new sentences that offer a more honest or clarifying retake of something you've written. Subject-verb-object format might help. Who did what to whom?
> - Go for a walk to figure things out.
> - Go for a walk to forget about things.
> - Stop for the day. Every essay looks entirely different in the morning.

Make Sure Your Structure Is Working

You have a thesis that might roll out at the end of your essay, or it might frame things from the beginning. Do all parts of your essay hang together around that thesis in an organized and beautiful way that holds the core of you? To check, tell yourself a little meta-story about what you have written to make sure your essay hangs together.

For example: I say [x], then I give an example with [y]. I question my assumptions of [y] with [z], and then I reframe the initial idea of [x], to show exactly how lovely I am.

An example with "Essay 6, Final," page 199: This student identifies a problem with sleep. He lays out some possible reasons for this problem. He moves deeper into the beauty of those reasons. He suggests a solution. Then, he extends this solution with another more magical solution. He wraps up with his thesis.

The problem/solution format helped him order his essay. You might try that with yours. What is the problem? How did you solve it? His essay went through many reconfigurations before he arrived at his gorgeous final. Throughout his process, he knew there were linkages between stories, but it took a while for him to make them. Be patient with yourself. The structure will come if you continue to work on the problem.

Sometimes, when you write the story of your life, you rearrange the chunks and seek reasons for your experiences to such an extent that you might feel like you're not sure if it's even you anymore. You may come up with a narrative of your experiences that feels new and the new might feel confusing: *Wait, did my family really play such a big part in getting my sleep patterns changed? Was I not just an anxious kid?*

When you make meaning out of your life, it might feel new and maybe even uncomfortable. But it's also kind of cool. When you see a cloud in the sky, you know it is a cloud. But when you see a frog in the cloud formation, you see that cloud a little differently. Same cloud. Both things are real—the cloud and the frog you make out of it. We have these beautiful, hard, easy, complicated experiences. And we have these beautiful, hard, easy, complicated brains. Our brains want to find meaning. This process of making meaning is ours, just as our experiences are ours. When you write your essay, you are creating meaning. Find comfort in the beauty you create from your life. You can make and remake your stories. And you can let them go when they don't serve you anymore.

Fill in the Blanks

Go through the questions in your online application and get them just right! It might be helpful to fill in the blanks with your high school transcript in front of you. You can likely pick one up from your guidance counselor, which is great timing because you should visit them this week anyway. You can ask them if they need any more information from you to help with your recommendation letter. You might even bring your guidance counselor a copy of your essay!

As you fill in the blanks, double-check every detail. Make sure you spell your name correctly. Sometimes the easiest things are also the easiest to mess up because you aren't paying attention. If you have to input grades, make sure you input them *exactly* as you received them. When you record your GPA, copy from your transcript and be as precise as you can be. As you get into the specifics of the colleges you have selected, make sure you choose the correct campus. People unintentionally choose the wrong campus all the time! Don't let a wrong-box click change the course of your life!

We all fill out so many forms throughout our lifetimes. We have become experts at quick. But let this process be a little slow. Breathe. Recognize what you're doing. You are placing your next step. Enjoy it.

As you move through the application portal, look at the essay prompts. Figure out how your principal essay fits. You might be surprised to see that it fits into a few categories. Writing and thinking are so flexible! Tweak your thesis so it fits a prompt perfectly. If the fit is a stretch, you can pick the option that gives you an open choice. When and if you apply to other schools that don't use the Common App or Coalition App, you can repurpose your writing. As you apply to different schools, later on the timeline, you can continue to shape your essay, reposting each time.

Prepare for Supplemental Essays and the Activities Section

Next week we'll start flying on these. But for now, just follow these easy steps:

1. Create a document. At the top, paste your current essay.

2. Underneath, write "Activities" and make a list of all the ways you spend your time. If you completed a resume back in week 2 or at some other time in your life, find that resume and copy your activities, extracurriculars, and skills into this

document. Add to the list! Include all the things you do—paid and unpaid, voluntary and mandatory, helpful and not so helpful, time consuming and not so time consuming.

3. Put numbers next to these activities, ordering them in importance.

4. Then write down the name of each college to which you are applying. Next to the name, write a date, one week before the due date (to give yourself some flexibility as you rush to the end). Highlight this date.

5. Arrange the schools in due date order.

6. Underneath each college, copy and paste each supplemental essay for that school. Read those essay prompts.

7. Reread the supplemental essay prompts for the soonest due dates. Your brain will start to cook on them now. Look at them before you go to sleep. Your sleeping brain can think on them for a bit. As ideas come to you over the week, write them down in your notes on your phone or in your calendar. Text them to yourself. Trap them in your brain and then use them!

Double-Check and Remind

Check your portal to see if your teachers and counselor have submitted their letters. If they have, write them a quick thank-you note or tell them you appreciate them after class. If they still haven't submitted, you can remind them. You'll probably have a pretty decent draft at that point. You could say: "As you work on my letter (again, thank you!), I thought you might want to check out my application essay." Or "I just wanted to thank you again for agreeing to write a letter for college applications. I decided I'm going to apply to Pomona! So excited."

There are more sample reminder emails in week 5, pages 86–87.

CONCERNED ADULTS
Be Supportive
Your person is finishing some things and starting some others. There are multiple projects in the air at various stages of completion and with varying levels of potential family/friend/teacher involvement: the application form, standardized tests, main and supplemental essays, college lists, FAFSA, college visits, recommendation letters, extracurricular descriptions. The beauty of this period is that now you know what you've got. It's in front of you and your student. You know which deadlines are approaching, and you have a vague sense of how much has yet to be done.

If completing a college application were like a good spring cleaning, you are at the stage when every single item in the house is strewn across a bed, piled up on the carpets, and spread out on the kitchen table. You are most likely, now, to stub your toe on something out of place or fall on your face in the middle of the living room and blame everyone in the family for your misery. It's a lot.

Your job is to be supportive of this "a lot," while also practicing some self-preservation as you step around the obstacles. Whether you're in the room where it happens or still anxiously hanging around outside of a closed door, there is space for you.

Keep offering; keep loving.

Help Your Child Get Sleep
They might have a final SAT or ACT this week or next as the exams usually fall at the beginning of the month. Sleep quantity and quality are directly correlated with test scores. Facilitate good sleep for yourself and your student all week (and forever). Talk about good sleep habits and their impacts on test performance. Turn screens off. Publicly commit to your own wellness. Envision your brain healing its stressed-out little self to make you a better person.

If sleep is hard, if you are an insomniac, if you have hot flashes that keep you awake, if your work and family obligations don't give you the time, if your neighbors are too loud, it's okay. Don't worry. You won't break. Your brain is a resilient little nut. Just keep trying or let it all go.

Sit with Your Person as They Complete Their Application
Consider the process of codifying oneself. Filling out forms helps you concretize your identity at one point in time. It's soothing to feel oneself or one's most important person in a moment, knowing that things are about to change. It's also important to make sure all those little blanks are filled in with complete accuracy. Two sets of eyes can be helpful.

Don't Sit with Your Person If It Feels Wrong
They can do it! Let it go if they insist. Pushing in probably won't help, but you know your person best.

If you are curious about the application, you can check it out on your own as a practice applicant. That might give you more of a sense of control. You can actually set up your own Common App portal to see what's happening there (https://www.commonapp.org). You can input colleges. You can make your own document that lists what essays are due at which university on what day.

Promise you won't get too stressed or too involved. Your student really does need to lead. But through your involvement, you can plan family activity or nonactivity around clusters of due dates. You can gain a better sense of how and when to support. You can empathize with the size of this mammoth task.

GETTING THINGS JUST RIGHT

Talk to Your Student about Extracurriculars

Last week, you worked on remembering your student's high school activities. This week, they are working on their list. If they'd like, compare lists and make sure they haven't left anything out. If they don't feel like it, just yell out the activities that seem most likely to be left out as they're walking out the door. If your person helps on a farm, cooks regularly with their grandfather, or does a lot of childcare, suggest these additions! If they planted trees once or helped their teacher after school twice and these experiences felt significant, they count. The little things are important and the big things are important. If your student started a business distributing bruised fruit to food pantries, how much fruit to how many pantries over how many days? They should be precise and specific. No need to exaggerate but no need to exclude anything that makes your person spectacular. You are helpful in this process.

Get Yourself an Extracurricular

While we're thinking about extracurriculars, now's the perfect time to add one into your life. Pick up a sport. Learn an instrument. Code, paint, write, bake. Take up the photography of trees, dogs, bugs, or people. Download Merlin Bird ID (the most fabulous app in the world) and become a bird watcher. Dance, garden, or volunteer. Play chess. Play board games. Playstation! Do yoga, meditate, read, or fish. Find a craft. Restore a house. Make a shed. Do a Ted Talk or watch a bunch of Ted Talks. Hike, rock climb, kayak, bike. Duolingo! Learn magic. Sew patches. Make robots. Carve wood, soap, or a good jaw line with *gua sha*. Dip candles. Shoot with a bow and arrow. Ferment kimchi, kombucha, or pickles. Play pickle ball. Hand-letter signs, notecards, or the herbs in your cabinet. Brew tea or beer. Figure out your genealogy. Make trees—ancestral, bonsai, apple. Geocache! Act in a play or a revolution. Collect beautiful art or scents. Keep bees. Trick-ski or parkour. Throw pots or axes. Throw axes at pots. Learn the stars in the sky or in Oscar-winning movies. Do origami. Hula-Hoop. Fly kites.

Buy a Piece of Equipment and Practice Your Activity
Yoga mat, guitar, carabiners, kayak, clay, yarn, racket, pan, guidebook, go! I said we'd talk about money every week. Invest in yourself!

Week 7, October 4–10

LOOSENING UP AND CLOSING IN

You're closing in, baby! You still have a decent amount of writing left, but don't worry. You're a pro now. Roll your head side to side. Dangle your arms down and shake them out. Open your computer. You don't even have to sit down if you don't want to; lean over that laptop. Blast words out of your brain into fabulous little snippets of you. Extracurricular descriptions provide homes for your most endearing characteristics. Each activity gives you an opportunity to write a tiny story about yourself.

As you become a better writer this month and through the rest of your life, you understand the power of a story to transport someone into your life. You have figured out how to question your quick thoughts and make them so much more interesting. As you continue to hone your essay, you will find that words get easier and easier to move around, to add, and to excise. Your own writing will start to speak to you: *I don't think you need me. You've already said this in a few different ways. Oh, I'm a sparkly delight of a phrase, say more. I am sitting here not making any sense and you know it. Do something with me, please.*

Trust yourself as you describe your life. Watch your words with wonder as they splash into new essay structures and tiny extracurricular paragraphs like happy little frogs, rippling out the most gorgeous portrayals of you.

STUDENTS

Honor the Time of Your Extracurricular Hours

You have lived this high school life in the best way you could muster. Maybe you joined every club and became president, chief, captain, or leader a dozen times. Or you're an activist, noting the unjust divisions in the world and then piecing them together. Did you help your teachers prepare materials, diligently, daily? Did you bag groceries for years with a funny coworker until you became a team, a force? Did you watch your brother when he needed to be watched? Whatever your path, honor it, with 300 characters across questions (50 for the position and leadership titles, 100 for a description of the organization, and 150 for the description of your contribution). Use those characters up until you feel your life complete. The Common App allows you to include up to ten activities.

Here is the prompt: *Reporting activities can help colleges better understand your life outside of the classroom. Examples of activities might include arts or music, clubs, community engagement, family responsibilities, hobbies, sports, work or volunteering, or other experiences that have been meaningful to you.*

The UC Application asks for a similar report, but it offers you more space! You can include twenty activities at 350 characters each. You will definitely find room for a tiny story in 350 characters.

Think about a moment or image from each of your activities that is most gloriously representative and include it. If you loved the bus rides to wrestling matches more than anything, you should try to include those buses along with all your victories (and maybe even defeats). If you started a Pokémon trading club, write about your favorite character, your favorite card, the particular sheen, or the value of that thing that makes your heartbeat elevate.

A description that captures what you love about your activity: *The $1k rainbow shine of a rare Charizard would be meaningless without the art that bridges my entrepreneurial aspirations with my little-kid glee. (148/150 characters)*

As you move through the "Activities" section, recognize the breadth available to you. The Common App people want you to write about your activities and awards and any "[o]ther experiences that have been meaningful to you."

Some activities might not feel worthy, but don't discount them. If you spent the majority of your teenage years staring at your ceiling, what was it about your ceiling that helped you grow? Did you heal, dream, play mental chess, consider injustices? Did you listen to music? Did you write letters or texts in your head? Did you curate your life, projecting an interesting version of yourself onto Instagram? Wonderful.

Write about how you spent your transformative time. Don't lie. Don't exaggerate. Just capture the beauty of your brain and your body in 300 or 350 characters. You grew and thought. With pride, describe how.

Use Numbers to Quantify Your Magnificence

If you nearly remade the world, you worked so hard, you volunteered your butt off, you led, you wrote, you scored, and then you did homework all night long, honor that service and that energy. Make sure you quantify the number of people, miles, families, meals, baskets, dollars. Were you ranked? Did you facilitate growth? How much?

If you look at your write-up and think, *wow, it felt like more than that*, keep writing until you catch the feeling. Each extracurricular should feel like a mini-essay that reflects back the energy you put in.

If you have a special talent that has made you among the best in your school, the best in your state, the best in the world, you must quantify it! Seek the numbers out if they aren't obvious.

One student was at first unsure of the application value of his video game habit before realizing he had actually acquired some remarkable skill. He recognized that he needed to quantify his skill, so he joined a few tournaments until he could pinpoint his rank. Top .3 percent in the world! Another student was an amazing leader of a remarkable set of cross country and track teams, though she wasn't super speedy herself. She quantified her magnificence by focusing on the leadership rather than the running.

> **Description with quantification:** *Captained 6 teams of ~50 and ~100 girls through 1000s of bonding miles and 6 state victories; transitioned team to socially distant fun during COVID. (150 characters)*

Use Precise or Unexpected Verbs

Organized, Coordinated, Initiated, Founded, Created, Developed, Established, Managed, Facilitated, Spearheaded, Collaborated, Implemented, Directed, Promoted, Produced, Orchestrated, Volunteered, Fundraised, Advocated, Mentored, Inspired, Innovated, Designed, Trained, Educated, Presented, Represented, Participated, Contributed, Assisted, Supported, Engaged, Empowered, Resolved, Researched, Performed, Demonstrated, Enhanced, Championed, Galvanized, Ignited, Harmonized, Crafted, Catalyzed, Energized, Envisioned, Exemplified, Stimulated, Trailblazed, Diversified, Transformed, Amplified, Revolutionized, Cultivated. There are so many more.

> **Description with unexpected verbs:** *Scooping ice cream, mixing milkshakes, hot fudging sundaes, and cleaning furiously teach me the value of service, communication, effort, and money. (148/150 characters)*

Consider Your Leadership Broadly

There are many ways to lead. You don't need to be a team captain or a quarterback to lead. Do you sing lead vocals in a rock band? Lead the rhythm of the people through your drums? Do you set the table, patiently teaching your brothers to do the same, leading them into adulthood?

Now, if you are a slack table setter, don't include it. But if you lead your younger siblings to help out around the house in a way that is quite sweet and consistent, write about it if you have space. If you are supposed to help with the chickens on your farm but you forget, you get too busy, or you aren't that great about it, don't include it. But if you sometimes find birds that have been attacked and you clean up those dead chickens so your emotionally attached mother doesn't have to, then that's a decent way of being an empathetic leader of your family. Griever in chief? That's something. If an activity feels important to you and might be considered leadership, include it. You might not be able to think of anything right away. That's okay. But work on it a bit. Consider what it feels like to be proud. Leadership and good work are often followed with pride. Write beautifully about the moments you have felt proud. A little vignette for your extracurriculars is the perfect way to showcase the tiny moments that have made your life. Ask other people why they are proud of you.

> **Example of broadly construed but true leadership:** *You take part in Quiz Bowl, but your team isn't great. You know your history trivia, though, and you love it. Your team acknowledges that you are the proven best in this subject area!*
> **Position:** *Quiz Bowl history team expert and study leader (46/50 characters)*
> **Description:** *Hours of trivia after school provide me with fun, relaxation, socialization, and knowledge. When a history category comes up, the crowd goes silent. (149/150 characters)*

Consider Short-Lived, Less Important, and Past Activities

These activities make up your life. Should you include field hockey, even though you totally sucked for three full years? Probably. How bad were you? It could be funny. Consider each activity a tiny essay in which you capture with grace, strength, or humor, exactly what you did and why it was important.

> **Example for a short-lived activity:** *You looked for asteroids twice at your local science center.*
> **Description:** *A brief but incredible opportunity! Analyzed satellite imagery to chart known asteroids and discover new asteroids. I found one! Sent data to NASA. (148/150 characters)*
>
> **Examples with humor:** *You ran track for years, never becoming remarkable and never winning, but you worked so hard.*
> **Description:** *I push my legs as hard as they can go until they cannot support my body anymore; the track then takes over in an aggressive manner. Many scars. (143/150 characters)*

And another:

> **Description:** *As Ariana Grande might say, running around a crowded indoor track with poor air circulation during a pandemic taught me love, patience, and pain. (146/150 characters*
>
> **Example of a past activity brought present:** *The Common App asks for activities that you have participated in during high school years; they want to know if you were in ninth, tenth, eleventh, and/or twelfth grade when you were involved. But what if gardening was always really important to you all through middle school? You helped your grandfather until he became too ill. You haven't gardened once in high school but you really miss it. If this activity feels significant, start your own plot right now. And then write about its historic hold on you.*

LOOSENING UP AND CLOSING IN

Group Activities to Save Space and Demonstrate Passion
You may find that you have more than ten things you want to write about, though there are only ten spots allotted for your activities in the Common App. You can group certain activities together to maximize the information you convey about yourself. Were you in the National Honor Society as well as honor societies for math, English, science, and art? If you want to do more with your space, group them. Alternatively, keep them separate if they are meaningful in different ways.

> **An example of grouping activities to make room:**
> **Organization:** *Central High School National Honor Society, Math Honor Society, Science Honor Society (86/100 characters)*
> **Description:** *I relish in the scholarly traditions, but more, I love the service. I tutor, clean up my community, plant trees, make blankets, and collect resources. (149/150 characters)*

Colleges love to see students who get involved and have a breadth of activities to show for this willingness to engage, but they are equally and perhaps even more interested in seeing that you have followed some passion, that you have intentionally moved toward the things that interest you. Through your extracurriculars, you can demonstrate that there are some themes.

It can be more impressive to list four or five related activities that show you have pursued a passion, than to list ten high-end, unrelated activities. Follow your own story and connect the activities if possible. You may be so naturally drawn to things that float around a particular passion, you don't even notice that there is a theme to your goings and doings.

If you don't see a passion that breaks through as you record your activities, don't sweat it. You are young. There are still so many doors that you might want to walk through to find beauty and wonder. No sense shutting any doors. But if you happen to walk through the same door a few times, highlight it!

An example of related activities that could show a passion: *You frequently attend car shows, you rebuilt the motor on you grandpa's Corvette, you worked ten hours a week to save for your own car, which you now dote on as if it were a baby. These three activities positioned closely to one another will demonstrate that you follow your passions. You might not consider writing about the car shows or talking about your motivation to work, but grouping these experiences in this way shows passion.*
Description: *Every Saturday I work with my grandpa as he finds and fixes old cars. I know good models, the mechanics of engines, and all my grandpa's stories. (146/150 characters)*
Description: *I've attended fourteen classic and custom car shows throughout the Midwest. Talking with car people, I connect across generations through shared passion. (148/150 characters)*
Description: *Grabbing up shifts at Black Hog BBQ, I worked my way to manager and also to a beat-up '94 Mazda Miata begging for TLC. I love my job and my car. (145/150 characters)*

Another example: *If you are fascinated with the number of habitable planets in the universe, demonstrate this passion by elaborating on the theme in your converging descriptions.*
Description: *My science fair project described and amended the Seager equation. I even reached out to Dr. Seager with questions about biosignature gasses. (118/150 characters)*
Description: *I took multivariable calculus at my local community college because this math is critical for a career in astrophysics. (86/150 characters)*

Description: *As vice president of the Science National Honor Society, I hosted three roundtable conversations on the possibility of extraterrestrial existence. (137/150 characters)*

If you have reached seven great extracurricular activities and can't think of anything else, just stop. Seven is great. After you complete your extracurricular section, transfer all your activities to your resume! This material is golden.

Add One More Story to Your Essay, Then Distribute

Up to this point, I hope you have been adding, adding, adding, adding words. Your essay might be very long now. You need a lot of material so that you can begin whittling down to something truly beautiful.

You may have been shifting chunks of your writing onto another document—a little home for temporarily abandoned thoughts. Maybe you cleansed yourself of these words and are feeling a bit comfortable, just a few words above or a few words below the required number. If you are a few words below, you have room for another story. A little two-sentence gem. Go ahead. Don't worry. You're probably thinking, *But the word count!?!* Forget about it for just one more minute. Your goal is to get your whole beautiful life into this essay. Add a little more.

Then, hand it to three different people. Tell them you need to cut one hundred words. See what they do. It's interesting to see what other people find unnecessary. I'll give you tips on how to do your own cuts in week 8.

CONCERNED ADULTS
Help Your Person Cut Words

Your student may hand you their essay to read for the first or second or seventh time. Lovingly receive that essay. When they tell you that the essay contains twice the number of words allowed, don't flinch. Maintain a passive and confident expression. Say, "Oh, okay. No problem." Help your student identify things they've said twice. Find sentences that are too obvious and therefore unnecessary. If a sentence has many phrases, ask them to divide it into two parts. If a sentence is confusing, suggest that they reword it—start with the noun and then follow with the verb. Eliminate any words that don't add meaning.

But more critically, underline, circle, draw arrows, and make comments in the margins about things you love. We all learn better this way. In every paragraph: *I love this! This is great! OMG. Funny! This is so you! I am proud of you. This made me cry. This is my heart. So important. Well worded. You write beautifully. This draft is great. This reminds me of . . . I never considered this. I want to hear more! So grateful for your thoughts. I love you!*

You decide if it's best to help through editing tools on Word or Google Docs, on paper, or through a conversation. Though you know your student best, the process might be easiest if you edit the essay separately. Writing is so vulnerable. Digesting criticism and receiving compliments might need space.

You are giving your person a gift with your thoughts and marks on their page or screen. Gift giving, at its best, expects nothing in return. Your child might not seem to appreciate you or even take your advice, in this or in other arenas. That's okay. You're a good adult. They are a good young person.

Edit the Extracurriculars

If they will allow you, read through your person's extracurricular section. Is the life that you've seen them live represented in the list? If something needs more oomph, indicate it. "Since you were a baby, I've watched you throw your whole dramatic self into musical theater. You list it here, but I think you can make it bigger." Young people often miss the amazingness of their path. What a wonderful opportunity to tell them how inspired you are by their talents and how proud you are of their effort. And get them to make it stronger so colleges will accept them!

Extracurricular writing becomes stronger through powerful verbs (*ignited, revolutionized, softened, complicated*), tiny stories (*encouraged soggy runners through streams and rainy hills*), and numbers (*propelled thirty-two runners through five thousand miles and two state championships*). Because space is limited, it's okay to use abbreviations.

Consider a Money Plan

Making a precise money plan is tricky. Many people will tell you that you must have a plan. And you will try to make one. Maybe you have been working on this plan for years. But there are so many variables, so many different systems, so many family cultures, and so many future unknowns that you may find this precise plan elusive. Your inability to find a comprehensive set of instructions will probably be pretty troubling, especially because there will be moments in this experience when you doubt that your family can afford college at all.

But you aren't alone. You're right on track until our institutions get it together and figure out how to make education affordable for a wider range of people. So considering the near inevitability that this will be frustrating, here is what you can do to make it bearable. You can have lovely, eye-opening, and connecting conversations about money that will allow you to become closer to your family members as you collectively dream the possibilities. Once your financial package arrives, usually with an acceptance email or a few days after an acceptance, you will have a sense, at the least, of the directions you might turn.

Have a Family Money Culture Conversation
Money Culture Questions

- How do you handle your money now?
- How were your raised to buy, spend, and depend?
- What has left you with a feeling of security?
- What makes you feel financially desperate?
- How do you feel about loans (of any kind)?
- Are you diligent about paying things off, or is this tricky?
- Do you feel confident that you can find money when you're low?
- Do you have a track record of making it through money shortages without significant problems or stress?
- Do you have a broader family network that makes you feel financially secure?
- Do you have a family history that makes you feel particularly insecure?
- Does your partner or do your other family members share or differ in their financial upbringings?
- What is your financial relationship like with your prospective college student?
- How do they see their current economic situation? Their future economic situation? Your future economic situation?
- How do you think these family factors will impact the money that moves toward colleges?

Make Peace with Your Economic Preparations and Situation

Have you been prudently responsible? You have saved from the beginning with special accounts that grow your investments. You have instilled in your young people an early sense of fiscal responsibility. You're working on the FAFSA, getting it just right. You have located schools that are known to give lots of need-based aid, and you have found schools that are generous with merit-based aid.

Conversely, are you new to this worry? You haven't saved much for college or prepared much at all. Maybe you are just trying to get by, and you don't have a single extra cent or second. Maybe you have a bit of money but just don't live so far into the future. You have consciously or subconsciously postponed this money thinking until now.

College is possible either way. And things start to get weird either way. You'll begin to hear that sending a person to school is impossible if you have no money. It isn't. As I've said, many people go to top universities for free. Please, if your student works very hard and is whip smart, apply high with zero expectations. Getting into a top university is near impossible, but if it works, it's pretty cool and highly affordable. There are also many smaller universities out there that are desperate to attract students so they can keep their doors open.

If you have saved plenty of money or if you make lots of money so that college expenses feel doable, you may still feel immensely uncomfortable because even the best accountants disagree on how you should most painlessly feed vast amounts of money to these voracious institutions. You might notice that, as you fill out your FAFSA, the institutions are assessing all of those savings in order to decide how much money they will give you. It might feel unfair, like your hard-earned savings are making college more expensive for you. But the best minds on this stuff agree, that saving for college is good. So don't sweat it.

We live in a stressful little world with so many responsibilities. Did you do your best? Great.

Discuss Financial Responsibility and Its Implications

Your thoughts and decisions on where your student goes to school and how the finances of that decision will be managed might arise from your own educational and financial history. Be aware of that past as you make your decisions.

I come from a world in which money felt abundant, though we didn't always have a ton of it. When I needed a few extra dollars, it would somehow appear through my dad. Sometimes he'd literally drop a bill at my feet and turn away as if it were an errant twenty, like his dad had done for him. I never felt guilty about that money I was given and I tried to be responsible with it. Once a year, my mom would take me shopping for a first-day-of-school outfit. I never really considered how much those clothes cost because she would direct me toward beautiful things that we could afford. I participated in tons of activities without much concern for their cost. I went to our flagship state university, which was super affordable in the day. My parents paid my way through it as I started accruing my own money. I didn't even notice the transfer, when I walked away from their financial care into my own. My money path was easy. This ease might be why I feel safe with riskier economic decisions. I am, perhaps, a bit reckless, but economically calm.

My husband started working at fourteen. He took on financial responsibility early. He made decisions about what he could afford and what he couldn't, paying for lessons out of his own earnings, forgoing school activities for his work schedule. He is so smart and made it into a fancy private school with a full scholarship for tuition. He worked hard through college to pay for his room and board. He tends to worry more about money than I do. He is, perhaps, a bit more cautious.

Many students and families come from less economic stability, which can severely limit choice. Other families have all the financial freedom and choice in the world, a privilege that should be acknowledged.

As we send our young people off, we consider what shaped us, for better or worse. We negotiate our feelings of comfort and the lessons we learned as children with the comfort and experiences we dream about for those who follow us. Again, there is no perfect economic plan, but with reflection, you will find abundant opportunities to be thoughtful, brave, and connected.

Possibilities as You Negotiate College Choices and Finances

Here are some ways you might do things:

- You and your student decide on the sort of educational experience you want, and then make the money happen.
- You decide on your financial limits, and then make the fiscally responsible college happen.
- You and your student opt for community college for two years to save money.
- You decide on community college for two years, so that time and maturity can clarify decisions.
- You recognize that clarity and money are always going to be hard to find, and you decide on a four-year university with community college as a fallback.
- You want a four-year university, as the quickest path to growth and learning.
- You stay close to home, to limit travel expenses and worry.
- You see where you get in, and then assess the financial and emotional comfort.
- You want to be at least two hours away, to force/foster greater independence.
- Your student is responsible for all college financial matters: tuition, housing, food, extras.

- You will cover all of your student's expenses as they move through college.
- While you will pay tuition, room, and board, your student will take care of books, snacks, and spending money.
- You will give your student a weekly/monthly stipend for books, snacks, and spending money.
- You will send your student with a credit card and guidelines.
- You will take out loans in your name.
- Your student will take out loans in their name.
- You will both take out loans.
- You will agree to pay tuition, room, and board, up to a certain amount (the cost of your flagship state school, for example, or another thoughtfully arrived at or arbitrary number that feels right), then your student will be responsible for the rest through their savings, through special accounts from grandparents, bar or bat mitzvahs, quinceañeras, graduation parties, scholarships, and/or loans.
- You expect or require your student to apply for many scholarships, earning college money.
- You and your student work together to cover home and college expenses through any means necessary.

Problem Solve

Whatever your family decides and wherever your student ends up, the college economic landscape transforms through time. Financial packages and scholarships often only apply to freshman year. The FAFSA needs to be filled out every year, and therefore, financial requirements can differ significantly from year to year. Housing costs increase and decrease depending on dorm culture and rental markets. Consider transportation costs, storage costs, snack costs, and the health insurance offered by the school. Are student jobs widely available at decent wages? Will your student have time to work, or might their academic path, sport obligations, or extracurriculars make work time limited? Will your student need to take a semester off or a semester abroad? Will they spend too much money on Uber and pizza, depleting their personal finances? Will someone crash a car? Will your refrigerator break?

I list these things not so you think about them and work them into your plan, but so you have a sense of how many financial matters can wander about, sit down, get back up, and throw a baseball through a window. Try to breathe, fix them as they come, and ask the college for help when it gets to be too much. Never underestimate the secret stashes that a college keeps to help you through hard times. Use them if you need them.

Week 8, October 11–17

FULFILLING YOUR WILDEST DREAMS

This week and next, my dear student, you will turn in some applications. Maybe you've already closed your eyes and pressed send for one or two places, warming up for the bunch of applications that must leave by the end of October. Applying to college and then entering a university might be just one of many next steps toward possible futures. But my guess is, if you are still reading this book, you have dreams of going to college. The people who love you probably have those dreams for you, too.

It is lucky and good to have a dream and then go through the process of trying to find it—walking into fear, away from stasis, and toward some beautiful vision. But this is the thing about dreaming: you can arrive at a dream, but you can't really enter it. The dreaminess of a dream makes it unobtainable. It's definitional.

When we moved to our farm, people kept asking me if I was "making all my dreams come true." I wasn't sure what to do with these sweet questions—I didn't want to disappoint them, knowing that people project their own lives through the dreams of others. I was excited about this next weird and wonderful step but also pretty scared. The farm was more expensive than we could reasonably afford, the weeds were more aggressive than I had imagined, and the hawks kept eating my chickens. I didn't want to disappoint those people who put their own hopes in my life, so I hedged when they asked if I was "living my dream."

"Yeah, kind of."

And for you, my friend, maybe you don't want to let anyone know that you are terribly unsure of your ability to do all of this—to finish the applications, to leave home, to go to a school that might require so much of you, to get good grades there, to keep balance, to stay happy. Furthermore, you are probably a little exhausted. Maybe you just want to be a kid for some more time. Maybe you want to hang around outside, walk to the store, and buy a soda or some chips. But now you have so many people watching you, hoping, dreaming.

At this point, you just don't know what is going to happen. You don't know if you will fulfill any of those external visions. But you did something quite special. You have walked up to the face of a dream. This is brave. This is how you make a wonderful life. Congratulations, my dear. Let's keep going!

STUDENTS

Cut Words in Your Principal Essay

The keys to cutting words are slow focus, growing recognition of writing patterns and problems, and confidence. Once you appreciate that there are a million ways to say any one thing, you will have more confidence in your ability to cut, create, and transform. Once you see the value of these transformations, you'll appreciate the slow pace. But you have to start by just moving slowly—maybe before you see the value. Go word by word, until you fully understand what each tiny piece of your writing is contributing. Cutting will become more efficient and faster as you move through life. It's a great skill for great writing. Here are some tricks:

- Save a version of your essay in a new document. As you start to tear things up, it's nice to know that you have all of your original words saved, just as they were, in case you make too much of a mess of things. That rescue document makes it easier to wildly cut. Google Docs, with its fabulous memory, is helpful, but sometimes it's hard to skip back through your many edits to the one you hope to reverse. Track Changes in Word can be your friend, because you can see your edits on the page. Recognize your favorite security blanket and then cut, cut, cut. You can always go back.

- Search for the word *very*. Cut every single *very* (unless you are being cheeky or dramatic about something that is very "very"). Also, cut *really*, unless you really, really need it. Just find a better verb or adjective. While you're at it, search for the word *got*. Find a different verb. *Got* is almost never the right word.
- Slowly and deliberately search for other unnecessary words, overly general phrases, and pieces of writing that say what everyone already knows. Extra words just get in the way of meaning and beauty. Cut aggressively.

An example will help you figure this out:

Before: *I was nervous, of course, but I was also excited to step outside my comfort zone and try something new. Now I can say that this ended up being far more than a summer job for me; it opened my eyes to the world around me and gave me the skills I'll need to be successful in life after high school.*

During: *I was nervous, of course but I was also excited to step outside my comfort zone and try something new. Now I can say that this ended up being far more than a summer job for me; it opened my eyes to the world around me and gave me the skills I'll need to be successful in life after high school.*

After: *I was nervous but excited to step outside my comfort zone. This job opened my eyes and gave me the skills to be successful.*

Now, let me explain how I think as I cut.

- "[O]f course" doesn't say much because "of course" means *as you would expect*. So why say something that everyone expects?
- "I was also" is not necessary because the "I was" is repetitive. Sometimes, as we write, we throw in extra phrases that help our brains stall. That's fine. We just need to cut them once we've settled on our idea. Sometimes repetitive phrases help with the pace of the poetic feel of a piece. This is lovely, as long as you have enough words.
- "[A]nd try something new" is really just another way of saying "step outside of my comfort zone," right? It's the same feeling, but "step outside of my comfort zone" is better because it talks about both newness and the feeling it gives you.
- "Now I can say that" isn't necessary because you are saying it now.
- Instead of writing that something "ended up being far more than a summer job," say what it ended up being that was "more." We know that you have a summer job, and we already know that it was important to you. We pretty much know that people learn a lot from summer jobs, so just write the sparkly part. This person writes that his eyes were opened and he gained skills in the "summer job," but he still doesn't hit the specific skills or eye-opening ways in this draft. (In a later draft, he did. And he made it into many amazing schools, deciding between engineering programs and selecting North Carolina State over University of North Carolina.)
- "For me" is obvious, as is "to the world around me." When we open our eyes, unless we have a vision impairment, we

see the world around us. But what, specifically? This student might have been talking about privilege, the cost of manual labor on such a large segment of the population, shapes that emerge from hedges, or gorgeous browns, blues, and greens. All of those details would add so much substance to this passage.

- "I'll need [skills]" is unnecessary unless the writer were to specify how and why. Because we all "need" skills for virtually everything, we don't need to write that we need them.
- "In life after high school" is an unnecessary phrase because we assume that you are talking about the future. We don't usually need new skills for the past. You could say something more specific, and it might be worth it: "... skills I will need to design tools in the engineering program at NC State as I work to better the lives of laborers."

An even better "After":

I was nervous but excited to step outside of my comfort zone. This job opened my eyes to labor disparities and gave me the skills necessary to design tools that can better the lives of workers.

This version is nearly half the word count but says so much more!

Consider Your Principal Essay: Is It Beautiful and Complete?

As you cut words, I hope you find yourself with an essay just the right shape and size. Are you done? Does it feel like a great piece of art that captures you as you are? Read it again with pride, futzing at it as if it were your sweet baby—adjust, clean, and adorn.

In the days until you send (there aren't many now), return to your essay to appreciate it and make the revisions that your fresh mind sees as necessary. A fresh mind always finds something. You may have applications due in late December. Continue to return to your essay from time to time, adjusting the words to your growing and changing self and sensibilities.

Write Your "How Will You Add to Our Community?" Essay

Nearly every college wants to know how you will add to the group of people they assemble. In particular, they want to know if you will be nice when hanging out with that group. You must contribute something, and you must be nice. You can be edgy and pointed and all sorts of particular. You can be reserved, non-smiley, contemplative, and concerned. You can be disappointed and hurt but healing. You can be confused and worried but resilient. You can be angry and forgiving. But mean, disrespectful, and bitter will not go over well. Groups don't gel well around those ways of being. Standing where you are, reflect on your communities of the past and envision the communities you hope to form.

If you come from a community where you regularly experience only a few dimensions of diversity, there still might be many things about life you don't yet fully understand. You might not have many friends who are of a different race, who speak another language, or who practice a different religion. Don't act like you know about people who are different from you if you don't. Having one friend who experiences life quite differently from you is interesting to explore, but that one person doesn't stand in for the rest of the world. No one expects you to have the world completely figured out now—or ever. But your schools hope that you will be open, curious, interested, and nice. So be humble in all you do not know when you approach an essay about community.

Now write a story from your life that shows how you fit into that world. Depending on the particularities of the question, you might write about your race, your religion, your body's size, or your unique abilities. You might write about your gender or your sexual orientation. Consider times when your identity has pressed up against difference, a gradient, or a variable. Did you struggle? Did you learn? Did you shine? Be so proud of those beautiful parts of you. Demonstrate your resilience. Show what you can teach others based on your experiences in the world.

If there's something in your life that you haven't been able to talk about yet in this application but that is important to you (your life as a coder, a sister, a theater star, a church choir singer, an ancestor, a friend), you might consider running those unique parts of you or your life through this essay on community. How will you share your talents and your experiences when you get to college?

A conflict that you experienced might make a great essay because being in community involves resolving conflict. If you went on a long run and got into an endorphin-fueled disagreement with a teammate that ended with growth and kindness, that could offer an example of how you fit into community. You don't let friction impede you from acknowledging what's right or just.

If you acted out a particular role in a play that resonated interestingly with your own character, that might be a cool topic. When confronted with difference, you recognize who you are as clearly as you see who others are, and you enjoy the growth that comes with new perspectives.

If your diabetes turned you onto cooking, amazing.

If you sing biblical hymns beautifully, but you're not sure where you stand on religion yet, that might be wonderful.

If you're Jewish/feminist/vegetarian but not as Jewish/feminist/vegetarian as you think you should be, that could be interesting.

The same rules apply for these supplemental essays as they do for your principal essay. Use stories, details, and sensory words. Start narrow and be specific. Write long, then cut.

Write Your "Why Our University?" Essay

As you begin to write this essay, picture your reader moving through a million of them. If you are planning to attend a light blue university, know that hundreds of students will say that they love light blue, that their favorite sweater is light blue, that their eyes are light blue, that light blue is like a beacon of hope. If the university is mascotted by a little crab, suddenly people will love to eat crabs, find crabs, or be crabs in elaborate cosplay performances (actually, that last one might be good). Maybe stay clear of crabs or light blue.

Instead, be preposterously specific about what you love. If you visited the university, look back over your pictures. Is there something about the walkways or cafeteria tables that felt warm to you? Why? Did you sneak into a library and find a small wooden desk on the third-floor landing? Did you and your brother take a break at that table to play a game of cards while you realized how much you love him and how hard it will be to be far away, but . . .?

If you didn't (or did) visit the school, spend a good amount of time on the website. Visit the pages that describe extracurriculars, programs, and offices that interest you. Fall in love with the possibilities for your life. Take notes. Use those notes.

In week 3 on page 33, I described how you might find your major or a few majors that are interesting to you. Focus on one or two professors who have the lives you want to live. If you haven't already communicated with these people, consider it! Now there is an added benefit. You can write about the interaction in your essay!

Ask them a question or two. If they're geographically close, request a meeting. If you have an exchange through email, a phone call (better), or a scheduled visit (best), write all about it! Describe how it felt, looked, and sounded. What did the hallway smell like? How did the professor respond? Did they make you feel welcomed, scared in a good way, or awed? Do you want to be like them? Why?

Do you want to learn from them? Why? Imagine all the wild things you could do with your life! You will show the university that you are serious through your loving attention to its details.

Did you fall in love with the university as you talked to its people and went through its website? Did you realize that you must be there and nowhere else? Great! This is what should happen to you as you construct each of your "why this university" essays. If it doesn't happen to you, if you start to wonder why you're even applying, don't apply. Add another school if you're running low. There are so many places you might go!

Continue to Paint Yourself Vibrantly True

Inevitably, there will be many different supplemental essays if you do this project big and apply to a lot of schools. Some schools will ask weird and wonderful questions, pushing you to show your quirkiness, while others will ask questions that are pretty standard and feel familiar. Feel free to reshape and repurpose essays you have already written for other schools and scholarships. Each time you repurpose, your essays will likely improve. If a question is truly new, write new.

Some colleges will ask you about your reading lists or your intellectual experiences. As you grapple for and with more material, honor your path. If you read a ton and a school asks you to list your books, enjoy the experience of writing down every single book. Use parentheses to show how you lived through the words of particular books. Add your character.

Example of Showing Yourself through Parentheticals
These questions were from Columbia one year:

> *List the titles of the required readings from academic courses that you enjoyed most during secondary/high school. Max: 150*

Response: *Night* by Elie Wiesel (makes me feel my Jewish history); *Chronicle of a Death Foretold* by Gabriel García Márquez (which complements *Ficciones* by Borges, one of my favorites); *The New Jim Crow: Mass Incarceration in the Age of Colorblindness* by Michelle Alexander (made me feel eager to rework our country's systems); *A Room of One's Own* by Virginia Woolf (though I don't love the ending); *Crime and Punishment* by Fyodor Dostoevsky; *To Kill a Mockingbird* by Harper Lee; *Cajas de Cartón* by Francisco Jiménez (read in Spanish, along with a couple I didn't like as much); *Wuthering Heights* by Emily Brontë; assorted poems by Seamus Heaney (short and sweet); *Fahrenheit 451* by Ray Bradbury; *Lord of the Flies* by William Golding; *1984* by George Orwell; *The Complete Stories* by Flannery O'Connor (where is the boundary between her implicit racism and her message?); *Man Is the Measure* by Reuben Abel

> List the movies, albums, shows, museums, lectures, events at your school or other entertainments that you enjoyed most during secondary/high school (in person or online). Max: 150

Response: *Get Out*; *Parasite*; *Black Panther*; *Lady Bird*; *Star Wars* (especially *The Force Awakens*); National Symphony Orchestra with Joshua Bell at the Kennedy Center (I saw Ruth Bader Ginsberg there!); *Lemonade* by Beyoncé; *DAMN.* by Kendrick Lamar; *Purple Rain* by Prince; *Raio X* by Fernanda Abreu (I went to a Portuguese immersion school in kindergarten); *Chilombo* by Jhené Aiko; *I Put a Spell on You* by Nina Simone; *Junta* by Phish; *Illmatic* by Nas; *Simple Things* by Zero 7; *Back to Black* by Amy Winehouse; Renwick Gallery; Smithsonian National Air and Space Museum; Artechouse Innovative Art Space (had a room of infinite mirrors); Hirshhorn Museum (I loved the Ai Weiwei exhibit); National Gallery of Art (I'm friends with the blue chicken sculpture on the roof); National Portrait Gallery; National Building Museum (the Beach exhibit); Dalí Theatre-Museum; Picasso Museum; British Bake Off; The Big Flower Fight

If you don't read much traditional literature, talk about what you *do* read: instruction manuals, social media posts, bad poetry, shampoo bottles, graffiti, comic books. Indulge the reader with the uniqueness of you. There are always opportunities in questions to highlight the real you!

Read Through Your Entire Application, One More Time

Read it through with someone who loves you at your side. Your eyes may have become so accustomed to your answers that they will miss little mistakes. This is the last time. Don't skip the read through, no matter how exhausted you are. Imagine, you put all this work in! What if you made a two-second mistake that erases hours and days of beauty? Double-check.

After you click "Submit," the school will ask for money, so you will need either a credit card or a waiver. It might take a minute or two to enter the information. Allow time for the extra processes after you submit. Quickly, before 11 p.m. Give yourself at least an hour before the due date. A day is better, really. A week or two is great. But if the thing sends before the clock strikes midnight, you won't turn into a pumpkin. You aren't too late. Power through!

Hit the "Celebrate" Button

Many of these applications have a "Celebrate" button. Click it. Again. Again. Again. Again. Again. Eat something delicious for dinner or for a midnight snack. Honestly, I am tearing up, imagining you at this place. You have done such a hard thing. And such a wonderful thing.

CONCERNED ADULTS

Celebrate the First Application Submission

This is the most important end point in the college application process. Not the getting in. (Well, that's nice, too. I fully believe in celebrating a lot, so don't skip the celebration then either.) Your person worked so hard to locate their identity, to find ways to love that identity, and to imagine it into an entirely new context. That's kind of huge. A dinner? A dessert. A little present!

As Your Person Peruses College Websites, You Should Do the Same

You can look at their colleges to consider their potential paths, or you might find a college that is appealing to you alone. Search through the different majors behind the "Academics" tab. Even though I worked in universities and with people through different academic paths, it still blows my mind how many things people do. Consider all the things you still might do with your life. Consider pivots and linkages that you could build.

Keep Editing; Keep Cutting Words

Enlist great word cutters and editors if you're feeling insecure about your own abilities or your available time.

Help Your Student Refine Their List

During this stage, as students dig deeper into the details of each school, they may fall in love or out of love. Be there to process that experience with them, if it helps. Pivoting, even at this late date, is fine.

Your student might be getting exhausted by the essays. They might want to cut colleges just so they don't have to write 250-word essays. You can help them rethink that decision if the college seems pretty great and your person is in a desperate cloud.

Or maybe you know they won't go to a particular school—too far, too small, too something. You can help them walk away. Maybe you see their energy flagging. You can help them prioritize applications.

You might start to worry that your student doesn't have enough safety schools—schools that they will definitely get into. Help them add. If your student is aiming for top-20 schools, no matter how brilliant and perfect your baby is (1600, saved a small town from a flood), these are *all* reach schools. You might add more of this type of school to up their odds.

Again, if application costs start to worry you, ask for waivers, look for free applications, and remember that paying money now might save you money at decision time.

If you've run out of time to visit colleges, you can add now based on your hunches and visit when your student gets in.

Do Emotional and Logistical Triage

Your person is heading into last-minute territory. They might have two or three or four or five applications due in close succession (if not this month, possibly in December). Now is the time to motor, to cut out unnecessary activities, and to encourage them to skip things if they are going to need the time. Sleep is pretty essential for one to keep it together. It is essential for writing well and not making silly mistakes. There might be little time for this sleep. Acknowledge what you're up against and be a great cheerleader. There will probably be a little break in applications from the end of November through the middle of December. You all can breathe then.

Look at Your Schedule and Consider Your Fate

Regardless of whether you are an I'll-be-at-your-side parent or a more good-luck-baby-good-night parent, you will likely feel the stress of October, November, and December. I made my older children both swear that they would have their work done by the time the holidays came. My "I'm not going to spend my whole holiday stressing about these things with you!" became, "I'm only going to spend part of my holiday stressing about these things!" to "Maybe you could work hard in the morning so we can all relax in the evening," to a teary, "In a few months, you'll be in college, and I won't be able to hang out with you in the middle of the night anymore."

Hey, Maybe You Should Take a Trip This Summer?
Wouldn't that be the best graduation present? This is a good thing to think about now, as you realize your kid might actually get into a college and leave you! You don't have to go far if finances are tight. You could go to San Diego, Chicago, or New York City. Stay in New Jersey and take a train or ferry in. If you live in the city, go to the closest National Park. Or if you have the money, go to Cambodia! Or Iceland. You could go camping. Start planning an adventure. You might plan something that challenges you. As I get older, I notice that I have more worries right before the plane takes off, when I kiss my kids goodbye. It's so easy to get a little scared, to begin to close doors and windows into our beings. With each creak and wrinkle of our years, we become cautious. Rip down that caution tape.

WINTER

BEYOND FAILURE AND SUCCESS

YOU ARE EITHER DONE AND CHILLING, OR YOU STILL HAVE A WAY to go. There are many applications with supplemental essays due in late December and early January. A bunch of California schools have applications due at the end of November. If you are looking around and everyone is shutting their laptops with smug smiles on their faces, restrain yourself from aggressive feelings. There are still many students out there looking at four, six, eight, or ten more applications. Maybe you couldn't quite pull off any early applications. My friend, it's okay. You're going to do it all at once, a little bit later than many people. You can write, apply, get in, not get in, put your head in your hands, jump for joy, live so big for these months. In any case, the applications tend to get easier as you go. You're getting good at this. Keep writing and feeling your delightful stories, application after application.

Now is a good time to take a look at those stories. Some of the most interesting and heartwarming ones probably didn't seem that way in the moment. Our family loves to travel; we make it a big priority. You might think that the perfect beach or the most beautiful museum or the best-laid plans would emerge again and again in our memories. But we tend to talk most about the All-You-Can-Fly Frontier Airline Passes for $399(!) that had us eating beef jerky and Cheez-Its purchased with canceled flight vouchers and sleeping on connected plastic seats under armrests in C Gates for days on several occasions. Or the huge family fight we had at the Vatican. Or how we lost a child in the M&M store in New York City. Or how in Denver, we were all so sick that none of us knew that our littlest ran off and threw up in an airport sink all by himself. Or the time his brother threw up thirty-five times in one night (I told him not to lick his hands). Or when our oldest was a baby and she threw up on her daddy halfway through a twenty-four-hour overnight bus trip. Oh, I could go on! I don't know why retrospective vomit can be so funny! We are such good travelers and resilient little beasts.

Most probably, you will get into some schools and not get into others. It's okay. It really is. You have to fail a lot in this life. It's just part of the deal. The more you fail, the more you succeed. And many great stories can come of it. They don't always feel fun in the moment, but over time, they're really just fine. The most painful moments can provide the warmest, funniest, and proudest memories. I promise. And when you succeed, oh my gosh, hold that joy in your heart for as long as you can! This is what success can sometimes do: *Yay!!! Oh my gosh, all my dreams are coming true! Wait, what will it feel like to go to school in a city? Will I be able to make any friends? Will I feel safe? No huge green lawns! I won't know anyone there! I feel so lonely already!* Best to avoid creating your narratives around success or around failure. They don't have to be your drivers.

Live your life day by day, try hard things, eat well, sleep well when you can, notice the cool stuff, notice the not-cool stuff, don't lick your hands, and hop and dive like a little frog, trusting in the world and yourself to be okay.

STUDENTS

Submit One Application Every Few Days

Keep moving with the same process. Read the supplemental questions for the next application in your queue. Work them through your mind. Sketch out ideas with stories, details, and sensory bling. Then rework, rework, rework. Send, send, send. Celebrate, celebrate, celebrate.

Or Take a Week or Two Off

Sleep, clean your room, and catch up on your homework. I'm afraid you can't blow off your last semester or your last quarters. Colleges request final high school grades. If you drop a little bit lower than your average, that'll probably be fine. But don't let yourself believe in that option. Stay in the game, generally.

But also have some fun. Hang out with your friends. Eat dinner with your family. Be aware of your current life. Look at it as if you are floating above the scene. Take a few pictures with your brain camera. Things are changing, baby!

Double-Check All Your Portals

Once you submit an application, you will be invited into the university's portal for students who apply. There you will be able to check if your materials are in as they should be. You may need to submit your test scores directly from the College Board. Your favorite college might be missing a required letter or document. If something is confusing, call the admissions office. Be your best self on the phone. Say please and thank you. Be warm and wonderful, as you are. Your high school counselor may be able to help you figure things out, too.

As You Keep Going or as You Rest, Consider Stress

How are you doing? Are you feeling completely fried but still somewhat okay? Or are you wondering about your ability to hold it together at all? Just know yourself. Feel the feeling in your chest or your head or your toes and acknowledge it with love.

It's pretty normal to stress, quietly or loudly. It's normal for adults to stress, quietly or loudly. You'll see it forever, everywhere. And things don't necessarily get less stressful out in the world. They can get better, though. Whatever happens, you'll leave high school or home school and you'll be around new people and different people. They have the potential to understand you in big and important ways. Wait for this! It's coming. Soon, you may feel more like yourself than you have ever felt.

If things get too bad for you (or for people you know), there are options. You could just go to a little island off South Carolina, Ecuador, or Kenya and open a dive shop (I keep this one in my pocket—though I don't dive). You could get in your car and drive across the country. (After letting people know about your plan. Don't steal a car.) You could find a stream and watch the water go by until you feel a little better. You can talk to a friend, a parent, or a trusted adult. Here is the national suicide and crisis hotline number: 988. It is free and confidential. Or you can always call 911, if you can't remember 988 in a time of need. You can call it even if you aren't sure that you are in crisis. Crises tend to be confusing. The people who answer the phone will help you figure it out. That's why they are there.

Also keep these things in mind:

- Pay attention to your breaths. This is what people are talking about when they tell you to meditate. There are a million ways that you can focus on your breath. You really can't do it wrong. Taking breaths sends oxygen to your brain so you can calm your fighty self. Focusing on your breath also gets you away from fears about the future or regrets from the past. You only have now. Breathe.

- Move your body every day, if you are able. It likes to move and can move more than you think. If you don't want to run, take walks in bucolic, rural places. Or take walks in urban, bustling places. So much beauty is available everywhere.

- Eat delicious food. Don't worry about getting it exactly right. Just feed yourself. We are these little animals that have been eating and sleeping for as long as we've existed. We know how to do this without trying so hard. If you want guidelines, make sure you eat fruits and vegetables. Protein is important. It helps you get strong and feel satisfied. Eat cookies sometimes. Don't drink too much soda—regular or diet. Try new foods with your friends. Eat regularly with people you like.

- Sleep. Just make sure you sleep. Don't worry about it too much, though, because worrying about sleep gets in the way of you getting sleep. I didn't sleep for months when I had my first kid. There were moments when I didn't know how I was going to make it through. But I did. It was just uncomfortable, and I wasn't able to think clearly or drive as safely. I fixed the circumstances by having my child grow up a little. I sleep now. It's delightful. I'm happier and better at things when I sleep enough. You will be, too.

- Feel your feelings. They make you interesting. Your feelings make you understand the feelings of others, which will help you feel connected and warm.

Interviews

Many highly selective schools and smaller boutique schools do interviews. These often happen in January or February but can occur earlier if you submit early. They can happen in person or virtually. Interviews are a helpful way for colleges to get a handle on your personality. Interviews offer you a chance to ask questions. They are also a great opportunity for colleges to involve their alumni. It's hard to tell, school by school, exactly what the balance of importance is in these interviews. Are you the main character? Or is it the alum? As such, sometimes these meetings are a big deal, and sometimes they're less consequential, but you always want to try to nail them. They can make a difference in your chances of getting in, but more important, becoming skilled at interviews is crucial. You have been given an amazing opportunity! You will do many interviews throughout your life. The tips here should work for many types of interviews, though the interviews may vary in formality.

For in-person college interviews, dress nicely. No need to wear a suit, but I wouldn't wear shorts or sweatpants either. Dress like yourself but upscale. If you arrive before your interviewer, pick a quiet table. If your interviewer offers to buy you coffee, thank them! If you are in line first, you might offer to buy, though they will most likely refuse.

For virtual interviews, dress nicely and find a good background and a quiet space. The room you are using should be clean. Double-check the camera frame to make sure your interviewer can't see your dirty socks or unmade bed. Try to practice with the virtual platform ahead of time if you're not used to it. Your shoulders and head should be fully in the camera frame.

Often, the first thing that an interviewer will say is, "Tell me about yourself." Try this, really quick. Set a clock for three minutes and talk about yourself. Hard, right? Inevitably, if you aren't prepared, you will stumble all over the place, go on for too long, or stop short.

Prepare by creating a little narrative that includes your general path through time and a few of the most interesting and important things along that path, focusing on your high school years. Write, remember, and practice a couple sentences about baby to teenager years. Where have you lived? Did anything important influence your journey to this point? Write, remember, and practice a few sentences about the most important social, emotional, intellectual, or physical things in your life. Weave a few sentences about your personality into your narrative. Make a short, sweet presentation and practice it until it feels natural. Having a ready narrative is so helpful not only for interviews but for meeting *anyone*, really.

Your interviewer will probably ask why you are interested in their college. Have an answer ready. You've written about this so you can start there (with new words; they've likely read your application) and expand. Again, tell stories! Stories are easy to talk through because they follow time. Make sure you have one or two stories ready for this question.

Take notes for yourself before the interview. Make sure they are neat and easy to access. If it doesn't get in the way of your conversation, take notes during the interview. You can say, "Oh, that's such a great thought. Do you mind if I write it down?"

Have questions ready for your interviewer, not just about the college but about their life, their experience with the college, or how they made it through. "Can you tell me a little about your experience at the school? How did it feel to move through as a woman? As an engineer?" For all interviews, prepare questions ahead.

You might do a bit of non-creepy research on your interviewer beforehand. Definitely visit their LinkedIn profile if they have one. Read articles, briefings, or books they've written so you're prepared. Ask them questions about their work or their interests. Wonder about your interviewer more generally. What did they do after college? How did that path feel?

Smile, laugh, and be open, if those things are natural to you. If you are softer, quieter, and more serious, be soft, quiet, and serious.

Just make sure that you fill the space with you, your thoughtfulness, and your curiosity.

Write a thank-you email or card. A handwritten card can be really nice, but you might need to ask for their address, which could be uncomfortable. An email that evening or the next day is just great. Be very specific about the conversation—write about the part of the conversation you most enjoyed or how grateful you are for a particular piece of advice.

Don't Get into a School

At some point around now, you'll probably get an email message from a school or two, instructing you to check the portal for their decision. This can be scary. You can gather support or go it on your own, giving yourself a minute to breathe through whatever happens. If you didn't get in, it's okay. There are other places out there. Let yourself be sad. Give yourself a whole day. If people try to talk you through it too quickly, if they want you to move on and be fine before you're ready, before the end of that day, tell them that you just need a day. If people you love are more brokenhearted than you, weeping and throwing themselves about, pat them gently on the shoulder and then find yourself a quiet space away from the hubbub. Share your feelings with good listeners and then forget that stupid place ever existed. Until you go there for graduate school.

Get into a School!

You did it! You're going to college! Oh my gosh!!! Send a screenshot of your acceptance to an adult or a friend who, you can be relatively certain, will scream their head off in joy.

Now, imagine all the truly amazing things about that place. Research the town. Study more about the school. Fill your head with ridiculously extravagant, wickedly cool, understatedly interesting dorm room decorations. Envision the new, the potential!

Be patient for the rest of your schools to communicate with you. Keep applying if you're still in the process. You want a bunch of stuff in your lap. A few choices will help you figure out your best life.

Read Everything, Log into the Portals, and Be a Joiner

After giving yourself a day and night of feeling amazing—hitting replay on the acceptance video, sending screenshots of the acceptance letter to people you love, and envisioning yourself happy there among the brilliant—settle in for a bit of contented work.

Reread your acceptance letter. One of my students spent a week distraught after receiving his acceptance to an Ivy League school. He read the letter: "Welcome to the Engineering School." He didn't know what to do. He hadn't applied to the engineering school! He applied directly to the college. He ruminated on his possibilities for a few days then a full weekend:

> *I could just become an engineer? Maybe I could go to the school as an engineer and then transfer? I could call and explain the situation. Maybe they would rescind, maybe they wouldn't, but I have to be honest!*

Resolved, but carrying the weighty stress, he read the letter one more time in his search for contact information. Upon this more thorough reading, he realized that the letter was addressed to BOTH engineering students and those admitted to the college; he was welcomed into the college. This was a happy outcome, but he might have avoided the days of stress if he had read the materials more carefully.

Once you've found some peace with your rejections, reread those letters. Another student had no idea he was on the waitlist for one of his favorite schools. (They tend to tuck this information after the rejection gut punch.) He ended up getting off the waitlist and into this place that he had thoroughly mourned. Great! But he was already over it. Read your letters carefully!

Also, sign in to the accepted student portal and read all the materials carefully. Often, you can register for a free T-shirt or sign up for an accepted students' weekend. You will find information for that college's timeline, for potential scholarships, and for materials that you must submit before accepting. So many important details! You might enlist a parent or friend to read with you so your eyes and your excitement don't miss things.

Seek out the social media pages for your potential colleges. You can often find or even create a group for newly accepted students. In the social media friending and following frenzy, you can access profiles and personalities. It's fun to share in the happiness, but also it is potentially comforting and helpful to see all of the people who might become your friends.

CONCERNED ADULTS

Stay Steady

Dang, it's a long haul, right? On social media and in the street, your friends might be posting about their students' successes. (They tend not to post about failures.) They might have it all figured out. You might have it all figured out! But many great application processes must continue. Hang in there.

If Your Kid Is Taking a Breather in November, Don't Worry

It's the perfect time for a little rest, as long as they aren't applying to California state schools. Remind them to clean their room. Bug them about non-college things for a week or two. Watch movies together. Play video games with your person.

Be Curious about Supplemental Essays

If you haven't checked out the supplemental essays for various schools, you'll be surprised at how many different questions are still looming for your young person. Once their rest period ends, ask about the questions. Talk about how you would answer them if you were the one applying. Maybe even try to write one for yourself. Have a contest for the quickest 250-word essay or the most absurd essay. (This actually sounds fun to me. I recognize that it probably will sound absolutely dreadful to everyone else.)

Consider a Visit to a New Category of Colleges

As your student has written essays and considered colleges, they have probably come to know themselves and their future desires more thoroughly. Revisit the college list. Should you add a small school or an artsy school? A nursing school or an engineering school? Did the winter make them think about southern schools? Did the social politics of a certain region make them reconsider? You're not too late to rethink or to up odds.

Understanding College Decisions: Acceptance!

Hopefully your student has been accepted! That's a delightful category to understand. Your student can go to college if they would like! No matter what school—one they knew they'd get into and aren't sure they'll like, a school you love but they feel lukewarm about, a school they love but you aren't sure about, or a school that blows you all away because you thought it was impossible—bring on the love.

Don't downplay any acceptance. There are so many amazing colleges out there. And this one might be the place. Even if you've started to be unsure about a college, figure out what is absolutely thrilling about each acceptance—the surrounding neighborhood, the distance from home, the light blue, the crab, the coach, the curriculum, or the indie music scene. What a wonderful thing to have interesting choices.

Equally, don't be too quick to send in your deposit. Think for a second. Stay open to what else might happen in this college application journey. Your student might receive an amazing financial offer from a different school. You might shift your decision. If you wait, you can use that financial offer to request more money from your favorite school.

The financial package often arrives within a few days of the acceptance. A global pandemic or a new FAFSA form have been known to mess up this arrival, so don't totally count on it. You might need to wait a bit. Additionally, many colleges require a few different forms beyond the FAFSA, so you might be receiving requests for something you have forgotten, missed, or didn't know about. These missing pieces might delay your financial package. People in college financial offices tend to be patient and thoughtful. Call them if you have any money questions.

Deferral

If your student applied early action to a particular college, instead of outright acceptance or rejection, the school might decide to push back or defer their decision on the application until regular action. Your person didn't get in on that first cut, but the school is holding the application to see how it compares to the other applications in the regular action pool. Some schools are fairly selective with their deferral picks, and there is still a decent chance at admission for your student. Other schools are less selective and push along nearly all the applications, rejecting very few. In this case, your student's chances won't be as clear.

Poking around on the internet, you can find crowdsourced information on deferral rates for particular schools. Just type the question into your browser: "What is the deferral rate for University of Oklatucky?" Reddit often shoots up some ideas. The information isn't always perfect, but it can give you a place to rest.

With deferrals, you may need to/want to write a letter of continued interest. I'll describe that to your student in the next chapter. You can check out letters of continued interest there, if you'd like.

Your student might be offered a different type of deferral. The school might love them but not have space for them that first semester. Your student might be offered enrollment for the next year, for second semester, or even for a special set of night classes. They may be given a chance to study abroad that first semester and then enter the home campus for second semester. These offers can come as a great surprise—not what the student wanted, necessarily. But they can be a foot in to a dream school. And, maybe serendipitously, they allow for more time to work, to mature, to go to London!

Waitlist

Your student might be placed on a waitlist. The college knows that they are a fit. They are qualified! But the school might have already accepted all the oboe players, quiz bowl champions, downhill skiers, engineers, and ebullient morning people that they can hold. Schools want a wide range of personalities, life experiences, and talents, and so your student's application was put aside.

Your student may have better grades and a higher SAT score but less impressive oboe skills than the next student. A university might go with a phenomenal oboe player with an ACT score of 34 rather than a mediocre oboe player with a 36. Of course, it's more complicated than that, but with this whole process, there's a bit of relative luck in the service of creating a college full of all types of brilliance. It's a decent process. It just doesn't always work out great for great students.

Let's talk about the waitlist. Your student will need to decide whether to stay on the waitlist or take themselves off the waitlist. If they aren't sure, stay on. Write a letter of continued interest, according to the particular school's directions. Again, more on this letter in the next chapter.

Some waitlists never move. Some waitlists don't begin to accept students for a very long time. And some waitlists are incredibly long. You can find vague information on your college's waitlist through their website. You can find imperfect information on the particulars of college waitlists through crowdsourced platforms like Reddit. Facebook groups about the application process can be helpful, too. The information you find from other people who have been through it might help you adjust your level of hope. But generally, don't count on getting off a waitlist. Fall head over heels in love with the schools that have accepted you.

Be aware of the stress that waitlists may bring. Your student might be invited away from a school they have already set their heart upon. This can be agonizing. My son was at his accepted student's weekend in July, filling out his class schedule, falling in love with new friends, in disbelief that he got into an amazing and highly coveted class, in awe over the beauty of the campus, when he received an email from what had previously been his favorite school. "Congratulations!" He was angry. He had no emotional energy left to even consider it. I suggested that he just check out the financial package. He glared at me. And we left it at that. Maybe he should have taken his name off the waitlist, but he really didn't know, until that moment. It's okay not to know, and then to know. He still loves his school.

My daughter was invited into a dream school. A dream school that adores independence and prides itself on its location, deep in a busy city. It was so thrilling and so grown up, and a little anxiety provoking because of this. We visited and found so much beauty, my gosh! She accepted their offer. That night, we had a lovely family party with light blue balloons (I'm clearly hung up on light blue schools). I bought a stuffed animal to hold the balloons, in a nod to her new mascot. We all wore the cheap school T-shirts that I found online and blue leis from the dollar store (you can celebrate big, cheaply; always buy balloons from dollar stores; or never buy them—bad for the environment). On the first day that schools were allowed to open their waitlists, three days after our party, her phone lit up in math class. She recognized the area code. The moment was magic. She goes to this other school now. Schools understand if you must withdraw your acceptance because you made it off a different waitlist. Depending on timing and the particular rules of particular schools, you may or may not lose a deposit, so that's worth considering.

The point is, accept a school on time and be certain that the school you accept is the one, even if it ends up not being the one.

Spring

ABUNDANCE

Whether or not you live in a northern climate, spring brings a thaw. A muddy warmth. Dirty floral softness. With the rain, sharp feelings can wash away, and you emerge, kind of new but older, maybe more mature, maybe happier, maybe at peace. This contentment could be due to the abundance of spring—flowers, baby animals, green leaves, and berries! College decisions?

Regular admission decisions come out during this period. These decisions can knock you over with their sadness and their gloriousness. I hope you can pop back up again, flexible like the limbs of a blueberry bush, filled with abundant possibilities.

Let's consider a blueberry bush and those abundant possibilities. If you are walking quickly by a blueberry bush, you might not notice the plant; you would certainly miss the berries. As your acceptances and rejections come in (the berries in this metaphor, to help you along), you might feel added stress when you think about the judgment others will cast on your abilities, your intelligence, or your work ethic. Be calmed by the fact that most people are just walking by, minding their own business, not noticing that your world is abundant with possibilities or barren and a little bleak. Feel proud and good about yourself or maybe momentarily disappointed but not ashamed. Don't worry about what other people think as they walk on by. They are a little oblivious.

But let's say you are standing in front of a beautiful blueberry bush, observing, considering, perhaps with a bucket in your hand. Suddenly, you see blues, purples, and pinks—berries changing color and texture for you and the chirping birds that fly all around! You probably wouldn't dwell on the not-yet-ripe pink berries. I bet that if you were to see these berries, you wouldn't get all hung up, sad that they weren't ready for you. You'd just leave them to grow full and beautiful for someone else. Don't dwell on the schools that aren't ready for you. Focus instead on the ones that are. Focus on the berries that are perfectly ripe.

But gosh, they are all so similar. How do you choose? Well, you'd eat them all! Maybe furtively, if they are in someone else's yard. But let me be clear. We're talking about colleges. You can only pick one. How do you maintain your calm while you choose the right college?

STUDENTS
Consider the Spring Landscape
These months are busy and a little weird. Not only is the weather changing, but the ground beneath you is getting softer, literally and figuratively. And the ground is shifting differently for different people, so it's hard to rely upon others as you work to position yourself with stability. The way you apply to school (rolling admission/early admission/early action/restrictive early action/regular decision) and the schools you apply to might walk you through different timelines, which produce a different set of emotional responses for every applicant. Here are some ways you might be feeling, just so you know you aren't alone!

Spring Feelings and Possibilities

- You have been accepted to a few schools, and you are a little post-excitement, starting to wonder what it might feel like to leave your high school and your home.
- You aren't *even* wondering what it might feel like to leave or be left, and you feel slightly unnerved by that.
- You are really happy that you will go to college! A few schools liked you! But how in the world will you make up your mind?
- You know where you want to go and are holding on to that admission, but you aren't exactly sure what it will cost or whether you can afford it.
- You've heard from a few schools but not your favorites yet, and you're starting to wonder or worry.
- You are still feeling fundamentally unsure, not knowing if you'll get in anywhere.
- Maybe you haven't gotten in anywhere and you stopped applying. Maybe you received a few rejections and you gave up because you're just not ready. Maybe you intended to apply but couldn't. Dear, there are a million things that you might do in this whole spectacular year ahead of you. Let the world spin once more. Work a simple and sweet job, take some classes that inspire you, go on a paid or stipended adventure working on a farm in Italy (World Wide Opportunities on Organic Farms—WWOOF) or blazing trails in a national park (Americorps, Student Conservation Association). There are many programs and possibilities—simple, challenging, affordable, extravagant, peaceful, raucous. Next year, you will be ready for a new world.
- Maybe you weren't ready but you're ready now! Is it too late? No. It's not too late. Many schools have late admissions, rolling admissions, or open seat admissions. This list of schools changes every year, but the internet will help you find them.

- You've been working and working on applications, and now, with just your schoolwork, you feel oddly available to do a bit more work. How aggressively should you apply to scholarships, and how likely are you to get them? Scholarships are abundant. Apply locally with the most fervor because those are most likely. Then put in as much energy as your body will allow and your finances require. The mathematics of energy in/money out really depend on your skills, your financial situation, your luck, and your persistence in finding scholarships that fit your abilities and your location. For a little more information and some resource suggestions, go back to week 5, pages 87–90.

Contemplate Your Acceptances

If you have a few acceptances in your hands, picture yourself in each of the schools. Your feelings might be different than before, now that you are in. When situations get real, they're easier to see clearly.

Construct a little game show in your head. Run the game show over the next weeks. Put one school up against the other and make them have little contests: Which school has the best financial package? Which ranks higher? Which will have better travel opportunities? Which will intellectually, socially, and emotionally challenge you most? Will that challenge make you grow or shrivel? Where will you find a cooler vibe, a calmer vibe, a sweeter vibe? Which school will have better coffee shops, punk rock music clubs, street dance scenes, symphonies, open lawns, or LGBTQIA+ spaces? Where will you be able to play club soccer, sing a cappella, or go to football games with school colors painted on your face? Which school has more interesting programs, lab spaces, art classes, or tech innovation opportunities? Will you be able to visit home easily? Will you be comfortably far? Will you be distant from those environments that make you sad? Will you be accessible to those who need you?

Make lists with pro and con columns.

Go to the internet and ask it, University of Minnesota versus Barnard? Duke versus GMU? Ask AI. Crowdsource. Read all the opinions.

Talk to all the people you love. Some will be very opinionated. Some will have no idea. Honor their opinions by holding them in your thoughts for a moment and then filing them away.

Check in with your gut. It will potentially pull you about. It might be an anxious gut, worrying about change, living in some fear. Try to fight the fear or float along with the fear until you find comfort—both options are fine. What decision will make you feel stronger? Prouder? Less regretful?

Take some time with your decision. Sleep on it. Keep schools alive if you are remotely interested in them. Even if a school is third or fourth on your list, it might be helpful to hold onto it as you consider the financial packages of different schools. Financial offers can be appealed, and sometimes offers from other schools are helpful for comparison.

It's still too early to let beloved waitlist schools go, though don't hold them in the center of your heart either. Those lists often don't start moving until May.

Write Letters of Continued Interest for Waitlist Schools

Letters of continued interest are love notes sent to an admissions office that demonstrate you still really want to go to that school. They are necessary if you have been deferred (maybe you applied early admission or early decision and the school pushed your application back to regular decision), if you have been waitlisted (they didn't accept you but they might later, if they find space in their class), and if the school has requested a letter (some schools don't, so you won't send one). Here's what you need to do:

- Read carefully the material that your school has sent you. They will describe what it means to be deferred or waitlisted from their university. They will tell you exactly what they want from you and exactly when and where you should send it.
- If the school asks for a letter of continued interest, and you do have continued interest, you should definitely take this opportunity.
- If a school doesn't explicit forbid letters of continued interest, and you love that school, send one.
- Your letter should start with a sentence that shows your gratitude for them. They read your application. They kept you around because they saw something in you. Thank them. Some schools hold on to nearly all the people they don't accept while others defer and waitlist a small percentage. You can find this information online with a little digging. These sleuthed percentages will help you adjust your levels of expectation and hope. As a rule, though, don't hope too much. Once you write your letter of continued interest, block the school from your mind. Focus on the ones that have accepted you.
- After your gratitude sentence, tell the admissions people exactly why they are your favorite school. Don't lie, but find one aspect of the college that puts it at the top of your list.

When I visited [University], I walked on the quad behind two students who were discussing Albert Camus. The dark philosophy in their lively discussion between the gothic towers reminded me why [University] is still at the top of my list.

In a back corner of the fifth floor of Walton Library, there is a little chair overlooking the engineering quad and Innovation

Hall. When I visited in September, I vowed to return to that cozy spot in the endlessly inspiring space of my favorite college, where I will think thoughts that make a difference.

Make it a quick statement because you want to save room for what follows.

- Following the same directions you used when writing your principal essay, pick a story you haven't yet told that highlights your amazing abilities. Did you win an award, save a life, or find new meaning? If not, no worries! Did you grit your teeth through a project or a recent assignment and produce something spectacular? Give them your new news or old news that is new to them in the most vibrant and interesting way. You have nothing to lose here! Go for it! Stand out.

Continued Interest Communication

An example of new news:

To demonstrate that my mindset is suited for you, my #1 school, let me give you a tour of my brain. You can see it at work here, in the construction of my computer, which came together in early January after I sent you my application.

First, I needed money. I reached back into my childhood of baseball trivia and memorabilia. I sold three Mike Trout 2012 Topps Chrome cards for $80, a Zion Williamson for $119, my dad's Garbage Pail Kids for $20 each (with permission), and another Trout for $17.50. Not a huge Trout fan.

I devoured PC knowledge. YouTubers gave me the base, patiently explaining the different parts, how to put them together, and how to set up software. Eating cereal late at night, I watched hundreds of other videos in increasing complexity. I experimented with component combinations on pcpartpicker.com. I bought PC books. I sat in the corner of my kitchen and read an entire PC manual to my mom. She pretended to be interested while making dinner, night after night.

On the sixth night of Hannukah, I opened the last affordable graphics card of the decade. I learned not only the economics of the baseball card market but also the supply and demand of graphics cards—an effect of a decline in semiconductor supply.

Before even touching a PC part, I could envision the placement of each piece. Although it took my friends months to build, I completed my PC in one sitting. I want to obsess over questions, projects, and possibilities at [University].

Another example:

I wanted to tell you about my most recent project, which didn't go according to plan (as most don't). I read a NASA article with a long-term climate change graph. My math brain noticed maximums and minimums at somewhat-constant intervals. Why, I wondered, would long-term temperature changes follow a trigonometric path? So, I tried to make the graph into a trigonometric function.

First, I needed actual numbers. I spent an hour locating the original data from climatologist Jean Jouzel. I found 5,800 data points. I spent another hour putting the points into a spreadsheet. Another, graphing them. I struggled to create sinusoidal regressions with

> so many numbers. I was stuck. I persisted (roughly) with gritted teeth using means, standard deviations, all the trig knowledge I possess, and plenty of deduction.
>
> My regression model was complete. I was overjoyed. Then, it got better. Analysis of the model brought me to my old friend: space math. Orbits follow constant cycles! I realized that the period of my regression model (the last 450,000 years) aligns with Earth's eccentricity cycle. Before 450,000 years ago, though, my regression model found the period to be shorter.
>
> Could there be other orbital factors? I discovered a debate initiated by Milutin Milanković, an astronomer and mathematician (yay!). Though my model pointed to eccentricity as a main factor for long-term climate, some scientists favor obliquity (tilt) and axial precession (wobble). My calculations corroborated that current warming is unprecedented and drastic. Math can find important answers. I want to live inside the problems at [University] and grit my teeth through the solutions.

Visit Your Lead Possibilities

If you are considering a couple of schools and if it is possible at all, travel to those schools. You might find an admitted students' weekend that sets things up for you and saves you some money. Fabulous. But even if not, consider going—especially if you don't know the place well. Ride a bike around the town. Tour some of the buildings. Visit a professor. Take campus transportation. Feel it all! The weather, the outfits, the buildings, the restaurants, the dorms, the grass, the fountains, the flowers, the colors, the joy, the stress, the vibrancy, the brick, the squirrels. Consider the openness, the kindness, the diversity, the inclusivity. If it all feels right, consider a sweatshirt.

Negotiate Financial Offers If Necessary

For need-based aid, call the financial aid office and let them know that you would like to appeal. They will tell you exactly what information they will need. Write a letter with an adult, perhaps, if they handle the finances of your household. Be honest, clear, and concise. Explain what they might not know about your life (a change in employment, a family illness, a hurricane) that makes the appeal necessary.

For merit-based aid, call the admissions office and proceed through the same process.

You should make all the phone calls. Not your adult. It is great practice and just a better look. They want to see that you are mature and capable. And you are! But they also totally understand that you might not be the one controlling the finances so they won't mind if you work with the person who is.

Make a Decision Slowly and Surely

First, you might want to take some pressure off yourself. If you are deciding between two lovely places with great academic programs that are financially doable, you have such a great situation. They could both be great in ways that you cannot envision, and they will both be challenging in ways impossible to foresee.

But if you gather your information carefully, follow your research and your gut, you will have no regrets. If it is truly the wrong decision, you can transfer. Of course, you don't want to depend on this possibility because it's a pain, but knowing that you always have future options helps you feel more comfortable about locking in.

Make sure you are aware of the final date to accept an offer. Once you commit to a school, once you are officially in love and you can make it happen financially, send your regrets to the other schools. Their portals and website will help you figure out exactly how to decline their offers. If you were in touch with an admissions counselor there, it would be kind to write them a short thank-you note.

You may be on a few waitlists. If a waitlist school isn't interesting to you at all anymore, now might be a good time to let it go. If you have a few waitlist schools that are quite intriguing still, keep them alive.

Thank Everyone

At some point in the next few months, once you start to know where you are going to college, write thank-you notes to your teachers and counselors. Write notes to everyone who helped you figure this thing out. You might even write notes to the admissions counselor at the school that you accept, as well as the schools you decline. You can tell them how much you appreciate their help and how you made your decisions.

A great thank-you note is a lot like a great essay. It uses stories and specifics. Your little observations and experiences are what will make your notes special.

You will want to put this off. If you write, "Dear Mr." and "Dear Dr." on the top of several cards right this second, you will be more likely to finish them in a reasonable amount of time. Just make sure you keep the same pen there beside them because you want the ink to match. That might be hard—to leave the same pen in its proper place. May as well just finish them up?

Gratitude makes you feel good.

CONCERNED ADULTS

Hold Space for the Little Pain

This year, my middle son tried out for the high school soccer team. We're okay athletes, as a family. But not necessarily make-the-soccer-team level. We're more like try-really-really-hard-and-maybe-win-when-other-people-quit type of athletes. But my sweet boy had a shot at a real high school JV team. I had all these visions of health and camaraderie and freshman social inclusion. I wanted him to make this team so, so, so bad. I talked to my older son—a wise young man—about my problematic soccer ruminations. He said, "Mom, you know, when I was little, sometimes I'd care about a thing, but not even that much. When that thing broke or didn't happen, I'd look at you and listen to you to see how much I should care."

The Art of the "Meh"

We can be as strung out as we want to be over our children's successes and failures, but if we want them to have a modicum of calm as they try hard things, we have to chill out, or at least act like we are chilled out.

We should all practice the art of the "meh," the "whatever." These responses may come in particularly helpful for you in this application season. They are especially good for long shots or could-be-cool opportunities. No need to dwell too much on these losses. "Hmm, whatever. You good?" Walk on by that blueberry bush.

Listen to the Bigger Pain

But once in a while, there is a college that your kid really, really wants, for one reason or another. It might be a college that you really, really want, too. My daughter didn't get into one of these in a death-by-a-thousand-cuts situation: there was an interview, a curious follow-up interview, a deferral, a waitlist, then nothing. That first deferral was so painful. We had envisioned, especially with the follow-up interview, that she must be close. The follow-up went great. We had all of these fantasies just queued up and ready to play out. That night was so sad. It felt to her (and to my husband and me privately) like a small tragedy, something we really had to mourn.

My gosh, thinking back on it now, it just seems so silly. She is so happy and ended up at a place that is so much better for her. You probably have a million stories like this—the house you almost bought, the job you wish you were offered, the love you thought was perfect, and then the house, job, and love that followed that were so much better for you in so many ways. Stories like these can be helpful. You might offer some to your child.

Or you can say some other things:

- *Life is big and unknowable, you can't even begin to guess at what that college would have given you. You don't know if you would have met the love of your life, found a cure for a disease, or gotten hit by a truck. Let's just assume you saved yourself from that truck.*
- *You did your best, right? You worked hard on your applications, made great decisions, and applied with such dignity. You are living your best life. Let's just see where it takes you.*
- *Shit! Well, they suck. I love you!*
- *Oh, I'm sad that it didn't work, too! But I've kind of fallen in love with your other universities anyway.*
- *Oh love, it's somewhat arbitrary at this point, right? More qualified candidates apply than they can take. We just didn't get lucky. Don't be too hard on yourself.*
- *How do you feel about it?* This is probably the best of your options. "How do you feel?" often works better than anything else. It certainly works better than "How are you?" That question invariably comes with a preprogrammed answer, "Fine." Just listen to their words and validate their feelings. Give them time and space to feel sad in the comfort of your love.

Calibrate Your Response to Danger

As your young person goes off to school and then even as they enter school, there will be hard moments for sure. As loving people in the internet age, an internet age that happens to correlate with an unprecedented rise in suicide rates among young people, moments of deep child-sadness may freak you out, as they do me.

When our young people are devastated, as they might be when they hear "no" from a school, it is hard for us to calibrate our worry and call upon an appropriate response. In college, when they feel lonely, bomb a test, experiment with partying and take things too far, embarrass themselves, make themselves ill, or feel ashamed, we won't be able to see their faces or catch their feelings. This makes it even more difficult to calibrate our responses to their pain.

It is very likely that your child is just sad. But if they sound different or desperate, if you just aren't sure, if you are worried, or if your intuition is alarming you, there are clear things you can do.

If your child expresses suicidal thoughts, call in a professional immediately. Call 988 to ask for more specific advice as you seek that professional. Nothing bad can come of this response.

If you are worried about your child but aren't certain if their despair is in a safe range, you can ask them very explicitly: "Are you thinking about suicide?" or "Are you thinking about hurting yourself?" Your child may roll their eyes and yell at you, "Mom, *no!* Stop asking."

This is what I get from my people. I wonder if I am ridiculous. I apologize, if I am ridiculous. But they know I love them, and they know I care. And if they do feel suicidal at some point, I will have given them an opportunity to express this. Asking opens a space for further conversation. Through these conversations you will be able to calibrate your responses more easily.

Our children must feel devastation once in a while so they learn to cope. It's important for them. But it's also our job to care for them. You are not alone in your worry.

Hold Space for the Joy

Even if you are worried about the price of a school, the fit of a place, or the distance from home, it's great to be joyful with every acceptance. You can address the concerns during decision time. Joy is a crucial component of a good life. Surprisingly though, it can be hard to muster. Our anxious brains and habits can be skeptical of the good, just waiting for the bad. No sense in this! Jump up and down with your person!

Once you have a final decision on school choice, even (and especially) if there are waitlist schools outstanding, gather the family, grab a fancy drink and a fancy dessert, and find a small gift—a dorm room poster with some Command strips, a toiletry caddy, a school sweatshirt.

Be so happy for this remarkable success!

If the waitlist school comes, fantastic! If not, it doesn't matter because you are already set and celebrated.

Visit and Revisit Colleges

As you dive earnestly into the decision-making process, consider revisiting schools or visiting them for the first time, if you haven't yet been. Before you plan anything, read over the acceptance letter and check out the college's portal to look for an admitted students' weekend. These invitations can be just for the student or for the student and their adults. They provide an amazing opportunity to be wooed, to feel comfortable, to feel uncomfortable—all very helpful when trying to select a college. These weekends provide opportunities to connect with other incoming students and to take ownership of a new type of life emerging.

You don't need an admitted students' weekend, though. You can go on your own with your person. Go on a game day, if that's your thing, and watch how the school and the town happens. Eat at the most popular restaurants and drink coffee at the highest reviewed coffee shops. If you have control, pick a weekend with beautiful weather.

Demonstrate Exploration

Embody your most curious self. Walk down side streets. Be drawn to pretty doors and high-ceilinged spaces. Walk into free museums.

Rent bikes and ride until you don't know where you are. Follow your young person, once they get the hang of exploration. No question too silly, no store too boring, no door too forbidding. Consider all the upsides. Have *so* much fun!

Demonstrate Critical Thought
Consider the downsides, too. If you are visiting the University of the North on a beautiful spring day when everyone is wearing sundresses for the first time though it is not even 60 degrees out, stand on a hill and imagine the bitter cold. Consider ice and snow and the gray that can hang around for months. If the school is a highly selective beast of a college, walk into a quiet library and see if you smell any fear. If it's a party college, consider the smells and the dangers. Walk around at night. Remind your person to never walk alone. Notice together if you feel hesitant or undeterred.

Demonstrate Openness
Ask to tour the gym, the foreign languages department, a lab. Strike up conversations with everyone you meet. Inquire about their experiences. Follow up on your initial questions. Talk to strangers. The ability to cold connect is crucial for new college students.

Demonstrate Your Love
Over dinner, really listen to their thoughts. Keep asking how they feel, what they think, and where they are now in their selection process. Cherish the moments together.

Model Good Decision-Making

Supporting your child as they pick their college can be totally delightful. You know each other so well. At this point, you probably know the options well, too. You may feel great about your money situation and comfortable with your roles in it. The decision might be crystal clear for all people involved, so you just follow your student as they lead you toward the best choice. Fantastic!

But often, there's more complexity. Things can get yucky when a student just loves a college but a parent is paying and it's just too much money. You might engage in a less-than-truthful dance, pointing out things that are wonderful and things that are awful, when the subtext is clearly about the cash. Best to settle money stuff either ahead of the thoughtful decision or with explicit honesty during the decision-making process, so you can be clearer on the factors of choice.

For example, you and your student might decide that unless a school's final price is under a certain dollar amount, it is off the table. You might agree that scholarships are a fair way to approach that amount. You might collectively decide that a student could take on financing beyond that dollar amount, the extra money coming in from loans under the student's name or from the student's savings. Or, as a family, you might talk explicitly about the weight on family finances. Is the tuition cost bearable? If the tuition cost will leave the family with lots of loans, in one way or another, are those loans worth it?

Beyond money, there are many ways to discuss college options. I've heard so many students say, "My dad really wants me to go to Penn State." (Maybe it's where I live but fathers seem to really love Penn State!) Equally, I hear many parents share that they are staying silent; they want their child to hold full responsibility for the decision, lest they get blamed when things go wrong. Both approaches are perfectly reasonable.

Whether you prefer to shout out your favorites, stay completely silent with your opinion, or behave somewhere in between, you have the opportunity to model how big decisions can be made by offering helpful frameworks.

- **Give it time.** All big decisions take a minute. Once your student makes a decision, you might tell them to sleep on it. When they change their mind, tell them to sleep on it. Note their joy, their resolution, or their discomfort as they settle into their decisions. "Aw, that thought seems to make you happy." "Stressful to think about that, huh?"

- **Make lists.** No decision is complete without several pro and con lists. You can add thoughts to both columns as they go, after they get a few things down. Try to appear impartial. Try to be impartial.

   I pretty much always know which way I lean, as my kids make decisions. I try to bet against myself, offering pros for my second choice and cons against my first. My guess is that my kids know what I think without me saying it—our children are intuitive little creatures and we're not as slick as we think, but there's some benevolence in voting against yourself.

- **Be logical.** Help your person research the statistics, the programs, and the services of the schools. Make sure that the school can accommodate their physical, mental, emotional, and social needs. If your person has serious health conditions to consider, this should be a primary concern.

   Finances often fall under this decision-making guideline: Which school will be cheaper in the short term, considering tuition, travel expenses, room and board, and cost of living beyond dorm life? Which school will be more lucrative in the long term, including likelihood of getting a high-paying job afterward, making professional connections, or having access to world-broadening opportunities that bolster resumes?

- **Be emotional, too. Follow your intuition.** What feels right? Is one place sweet and open and the other a little gray? In which ways do the schools make you feel anxious? Some anxiety is great—hard work, new people, and a different environment, which will help you know the world. Other anxiety isn't so great—not feeling like you'll fit in with the particular vibe or culture of the place, or worrying that you won't be challenged to grow intellectually, emotionally, or socially. Does one place feel absolutely right in the morning when you're brave and fresh and absolutely wrong in the evening when you're exhausted and want comfort?

- **Delve into hesitations.** Should you follow your fear? Your need for comfort? With all your hesitations, push yourself toward growth but not danger. Feeling over your head in hard work can be an amazing thing—unless your person knows that they are not able to healthfully handle it.
- **Jump.** At some point, your baby has to decide. If you've gone through a full decision-making process together or individually alone but open, you'll probably land at the same place or close to the same place. When this is the case, tell your person how much confidence you have in their ability to decide. Who knows if it will be absolutely right! It will certainly not be perfect, and there definitely will be moments when your student might doubt themselves. Tell them to expect this, and remind them about how thoughtful they were as they decided.

Shift a Little

I probably don't need to write this at all, except maybe to acknowledge that it happens—gradually and naturally. Things begin to shift slowly in the spring and the summer. Applying to college matures a person. Growing up matures a person. You might find yourself letting go. Feeling what it feels like to monitor less, to ignore triggers and old sticking points. See what happens. Feel what it feels like to just watch and to breathe (within reason).

Summer

THE CATACLYSM

Scientists speculate that the earth's inner core occasionally slows to near stillness and then changes direction. They assure us that "nothing cataclysmic is happening." The earth's center just doesn't spin for a bit. Then, it starts back up. It does this from time to time. We can go about our business.

Before my kids began to leave, I couldn't really imagine what it would feel like. In my head, I've always calmly envisioned the lucky inevitability. I have been excited for my kids to feel the fabulousness of young community, of dorm food, of hectic class schedules, and of stressful late nights with just the right snacks and camaraderie.

But when the college moment approached and then actually arrived, when I sat down and considered that her shoes wouldn't be there and her room would be strangely clean and we wouldn't need to cook kale all the time and she wouldn't be infusing that blend of adventure/anxiety/empathy/cleverness into our air, I became suddenly devastated. Everything would change. Our house would be three boys, a man, and me. Parenting as we had known it would instantly have an intensely different flavor. That feeling of indescribable us, that we know to our core, would be gone. Done.

I wasn't sure what to mourn or how to mourn it. The core of our world would stop spinning for a bit. I wondered if that still would impact our place in the universe and drop us into some pit of despair.

It didn't. Things just stayed still for a little bit, so that our child could hop off. And then the world started spinning again, maybe in a different direction, but the motion felt familiar. You'll all be okay. It's scary, but you'll be okay.

Students, even though the core has slowed to a crawl, that mantle is still whipping around. Focus and take a great big jump! You've got this, babies!

STUDENTS

Keep Simple Rules for Yourself

Though you are certainly already there in many ways, you are entering a world in which you have more control and more power. This shift might feel overwhelming but also might be liberating. There will be many decisions to make every day. If you have simple rules for yourself, it makes things easier. Here are a few, from my mama heart to your heart. Just follow your rules—these or the ones you make up for yourself. With your rules, you can be clear-eyed about decisions without stressing too much about outcomes. If you do your best, you do your best.

No Regrets

The "no regrets" rule comes in handy with big, little, and scary decisions. You will need to decide which courses to take, which friends to hang out with, how much to party, how much to study, how much to spend or save, what to say or not to say. If you put the "no regrets" part of your body in charge, you will figure out how to make decisions that push you effectively without hurting you.

Now, if you are on a high quarry cliff with a bunch of friends, make sure you play it all the way out. Of course, you want to live a big life (picture the big life, you jumping off a cliff—woo hoo, no regrets!!!). But please, also picture that this quarry may be dangerously shallow and jumping could lead to paralysis or worse. Picture that. Jumping can be the more regrettable decision. Big jumps are often amazing, but stay safe.

Be Relentlessly Curious

Be relentlessly curious about the world, about other people, about your studies, about yourself. There is so much to learn! So much! And the more you learn, the greater access you will have to all the questions of the universe. This idea—"the more you know, the more you do not know"—is attributed to so many great thinkers, Aristotle, Einstein, and you in a minute when you tell a friend. Because, if you haven't felt this already, you will very soon, and it will blow you away. I am so happy for you.

You will be sitting in one of your classes, when all of a sudden, the material from your other classes will begin to swirl in and the concepts will speak to each other. The foundational material of your freshman year acts as a scaffolding upon which so many thoughts and concepts can then rest. Your brain will be able to hold an exponentially greater amount of beauty than it could previously. As you begin to understand more fully eras and geographical layouts and scientific processes and animal behavior, everything around you will make so much more sense.

Lean in to the deluge, the gush, and the wild extravagance of informational quantity. You probably know the kids in classes from your past who ask, "When am I ever going to use this information?" They just don't yet get it—the way the information builds on itself to show you the most gorgeous universe, the most gorgeous you!

Be Kind

You will meet so many new people from so many parts of the world, with so many experiences, fears, tragedies, biases, and vulnerabilities. They will be naïve and wrong and right and true and in pain and in love. You don't have to formulate a different way for each of these types of beings. You don't need to protect yourself too much, teach too much, or guard too much. You just have to be nice. You should listen. You should try to understand.

Be nice to the material you learn, too. It is the easiest thing in the world to criticize a text, a pedagogy, a piece of literature, or a way of being. There are many ways to do things right, but there are many multiple more ways, millions times millions of ways to do things wrong. If you point out *only* what is wrong in your intellectual, social, and emotional perusals, you will be taking the easy road. Consider all the ways something is inspiring and right. Then, consider the ways to make it better. Find the absences that the problems reveal. And then add.

Some material, however, is kind of mean. Not good for the world. Feel free to tear this stuff up.

Be kind to all people. In my twenties, I visited Washington, DC, with a group of friends. At sunrise, we entered a park to see the cherry blossoms, which bloom breathtakingly for a short period of time in the spring. We had the beauty all to ourselves, when a line of cars passed through the entrance, shutting off the park to other visitors. The presidential motorcade approached. My friends and I weren't fans of this particular president, yet I could feel the warmth in his smile as he made eye contact and passed with his window down, just a few feet away. We were sharing such beauty! I felt that I had some power, in that moment, if he were to stop. We could chat. I could express my concerns.

But suddenly, I saw him become so sad. I followed his sight line to my friend, beside me, who was giving him the middle finger. It was shocking how one small gesture could permeate a person with such power. The moment felt tragic. Unkind acts, while incredibly strong, are not effective motivators. Kindness is among the most powerful tools you wield.

Be kind to yourself, most importantly. You will have so many opportunities in college to compare yourself to other people. You will inevitably see the ways in which you are better and worse. This can make you complacent and insecure. Maybe even ashamed. It's pretty human to compare ourselves and feel sad, regretful, and down.

But instead, I hope that you are inspired by the beauty and tragedy of others. When you are inspired by someone's sense of style, for example, don't get down on your own clothing. Don't hate the stylish person for their creative flair. Just approach that beautiful style in admiration. You can learn from it if you want. Go to a secondhand store and follow their artistic lead until others follow you.

Spend Your Energy (Or Rest)

I have this friend named Gordon. He is one of those people who can do so many things. I went on a beach trip with him and a bunch of other friends in college. The second we arrived, he started making a sand castle. Not just any castle—an elaborate structure that just continued to become more delightful by the second. He spent the entire day building this castle, while the rest of us lounged in the sun. It was a stunning pile of sand!

In that moment, I decided that I, too, would become a sand castle builder. As I've gone through life, had one child, then another, then two more, as I've visited many different beaches, as I get older and wrinkled, I make sand castles. I get sand in my hair and swimsuit. When I eat a sandwich or some chips on the beach, each bite is a little crunchy. I get uneven sunburns and I chafe, but I make beautiful sand castles. I feel their power. My children know their power. We appreciate the discomfort and the energy; it brings such joy. Gordon has made all my beach days a million times more amazing, and my pumpkin patch days, and my Sundays, and my Tuesdays, and my birthdays, and my trips to the store and to other countries so much more amazing by demonstrating how to use energy. He also makes sourdough pizza and pickles. He juggles and photographs. He can do little mime acts. He makes fancy cocktails. He is an engineer and a musician in rock bands. Be like Gordon. Your life will be full!

And rest! Once you are done with your sand castle, rest. But maybe you just aren't going to be making sand castles. Maybe your life doesn't throw sand at you. Maybe your life requires so much action, so much thought, or so much maintenance that the commitment you must make to yourself is to rest. This also leads to a full life.

Do Hard Things

Trick yourself into doing them by signing up before you're ready, before you feel comfortable. Sign up when the idea of the thing still seems so absurd. Right after college, I applied for this program that doesn't exist anymore called WorldTeach. They had a special opening on a tiny island in the middle of the Pacific. They requested a person who was good with isolation and who could get by in Spanish. I responded and assured them that I spoke a little Spanish (*uno, dos, tres,* and *buenos dias*—that's all, no more) and that I was amazing at isolation. I lived with the most wonderful family who became my family. I speak Spanish now, due to their loving patience. I returned again and again, once with a Fulbright, doing PhD research, and then with my whole family. They visited in 2022—thirty years after we met. Best thing ever!

I was a bike messenger in Seattle, though I'm not very coordinated. My boss told me that I got the job because I could spell. I once carried thousands of fortune cookies up and down the hills of that up-and-down town. Lots of legal briefs. I wore a skirt. Girrrrrl power. Best thing ever! Push your boundaries by expanding your skill set in interesting and odd ways.

And One More Thing

When you get too tired, no matter what else is happening, no matter how much you still must do, sleep. When you get too stressed, breathe, hang out with a friend, or call someone you love. When you are hungry, eat. Eat regularly, including fruits and vegetables. But don't stress out too much when you indulge. Indulgence is also a way to be kind to yourself. Count your breaths. Be grateful. Journal. Don't drink energy drinks. Wear sunscreen. Always maintain control over your drinking glass at a party (so that no one puts anything in it). If you drink alcohol, don't drink too much; it's dangerous. Love the way you look. You are beautiful! Become even stronger. Take lots of long walks. Walk with friends at night, never alone. Join at least two clubs right away when you get to school. Go to office hours. Get to know your professors and TAs. Call home when you get lonely. Call home when you're happy. Send screenshots of your good exams. Share your misery when you do terribly. Cheer for yourself. Listen to people when they are sad. Just listen to people. Follow your intuition; if something feels not right, leave. Go to class. Take good notes. Pleasure read. Gritted-teeth hard read. Get season tickets. Ask for help. Ask for extensions when you need them. Get a therapist; they're often free at most colleges. Push through when you can but not when you can't. Rest if you feel sick. Make sure you have your EpiPen. Avoid allergens. Do homework with friends. If you feel like you don't have any friends, OMG, don't worry; that's so normal. Everyone feels like that sometimes. Reinvent yourself. Or don't. Gather people who aren't perfect. Keep the ones you trust close. Join someone in the cafeteria even if it might be a little awkward. Give gifts. Live minimally because it's important for the environment. Live prudently because then you don't have to worry so much about money. But embrace abundance! Make cupcakes with sprinkles with your friends in the dorm kitchen. Stand up for yourself and for other people. Bring dirty laundry home. But also, get good at laundry. (I'm still not sure how to use bleach!) But don't use fabric softener because I heard it can make you sick. Be where your feet are—really in the moment. If your feet are on a high cliff or an icy lake surface, be very, very careful; please, promise me.

CONCERNED ADULTS
Take Action on Irrational Worry
Your child doesn't seem right. They are somehow more independent but also emotional or not emotional, which is so confusing. What psychological and/or biological issue is creating this behavior? Push them toward therapy. Take the introductory virtual session yourself, if they refuse. If and when they seem open to therapy after you explain that *everyone* should get therapy and especially teenagers after a pandemic in this internet age (and especially adults after a pandemic in this internet age), recognize that good therapists in your area are nearly impossible to find and insurance rarely covers the best of them. Wonder about your child's rashes. Are they having too many headaches? Consider genetic versus environmental maladies. Consider relocating to a new environment for a fresh start so that you don't break your other children, if you haven't already. Consider your own health history. Schedule your annual checkup. Find yourself therapy.

Throw Your Whole Self into an Extra-Long Sheets Project
Research thread counts, dimensions, colors, and patterns. Learn about mattress pads. There is so much to know about mattress pads. Their complexity is what makes them prohibitively expensive. Start hoarding Bed Bath & Beyond coupons for 20 percent off. Recognize that Bed Bath & Beyond went out of business, or did they? Make a run through Target on your own, scouting out sheet sets. No, go to Costco! Recognize that there are disastrously few Twin XLs. Panic. Note that your child is utterly uninterested, still, at two

months out. When you finally make it to a relevant store, a week before departure, your child will break down in the pillow department. Too many choices. You won't buy a mattress pad. Consider T.J.Maxx.

Give Advice
You only have a little time left to teach them everything they need to know. When you think of little tips, text them in the middle of their work shift. If you think of these tips at 3 a.m. while you are fretfully ruminating, enter their room wild-eyed; you might need to wake them up, lest you forget. But also remind them first thing in the morning because they might have been too sleepy to take in the details. They must understand how to be kind, how to stay healthy, how to work hard, *and* how not to work too hard. You must teach them about managing their own money, their sleep, their food, and their stress. Make lists. Send them lists. Repeat things with slight derivations in theme and content. Accent those derivations to assure them that they have it right.

Mark All the Lasts
Last basketball game. Last concert. Last essay. Last lightning storm. Last stop at Chipotle after annual six-month dentist appointment. Last time you buy them gum when they grocery shop with you. And then the last time again. Hold these moments to your heart and feel them, profoundly. It's okay if you cry, often.

Prepare a Scrapbook, Journal, or Picture Album
Wonder why you didn't start it when they were babies. Or lament the fact that you only got to page 2. Spend all summer making the best damn scrapbook/journal/picture album (all three?) that anyone has ever seen. Otherwise, they might not know how much you love them.

Make a Communication Contract

Consider that your child must make their own way. You understand that they will need independence. This independence might feel lonely from time to time. But they will surely need you. Quite often. But no more than two times a day. Three?

As you drive them to college, consider deleting your tracking apps—your Life360 and Find My Phone. No, don't bring up Find My Phone. Maybe they will forget about it, and you can still check in from time to time, just to be on the safe side. Like if they are traveling or something. Before you delete your tracking app, look into your phone screen at their little bubble with their little face. See them in the rearview mirror, head on the window glass, earbuds in. Your images, your bodies—so close together now! Sob. Stifle it. Turn off tracking. Practice FaceTime. Learn Snapchat.

Hook Your Leg Out the Door and Slow the World by Dragging Your Foot against Time

Let your child go. Tell them you love them. Run back and tell them you love them again. And once more. Then give a little push off with your foot to start the thing spinning again.

ADDENDUM ESSAY EXAMPLES

Essay 1, Final (UCLA!)

When I was five, I would sit on my *abuela*'s lap as she ran her shiny white sewing machine. We would sew for hours, stitching row after row of straight lines on the fabric scraps that littered her sewing table. When the basics became second nature, she introduced progressively more difficult projects, starting with bowl cozies to protect people's hands from hot soup and cold ice cream. When everyone in my family had a lifetime supply of those, we transitioned to zippered pouches. It was fun, but it seemed like nothing more than a hobby for old ladies. Why should I, a young girl in the 21st century, learn to sew?

In 2019, my *abuela* gifted me a sewing machine of my own. Soon after, the pandemic arrived and, with it, a demand for masks. I scoured the internet for patterns and instructional videos. Dozens popped up, all claiming to make the perfect mask. I recreated each one, triple checking my measurements. No matter how precisely I measured, none of the instructions were as perfect as their creators claimed. From poking me in the eye every time I spoke to being outright ugly, each had a small yet troublesome defect. It was clear that none of the online videos would lead me to the flawless mask I envisioned. So I set out to create a pattern of my own. I analyzed all the masks in my current collection and began to prototype. With each new version came a new fix for each source of discomfort.

My *abuela* taught me to design solutions. My mom encouraged me to solve problems.

I was raised on the call-and-response chants of workers' picket lines. Civic participation is in my blood. Every election, I sit at the kitchen table with my mom as she fills out her ballot, discussing the issues up for debate. When I flood her with questions about this candidate or that ballot measure, she takes the time to explain each, in minute detail.

This deep understanding of the importance of community participation led me to become a poll worker during the 2022 election. The first three days of the four-day commitment were long. I spent most of my time on the splinter-filled gym bleachers struggling my way through the *Scarlet Letter*, hoping someone would come vote.

When election day finally arrived, people flooded in. Through the chaos, I noticed a woman standing in the corner with a worried look. Struggling through broken English, she explained the difficulty she was having making sense of several propositions and the embarrassment she felt asking for help. In Spanish, I assured her the legal jargon of the writing made it tricky for everyone and handed her a ballot translated into her native language. I stayed with her for the remainder of the process, guiding her through each step.

Both my *abuela* and my mom have shaped the way I approach challenges. The prototyping I learned at the sewing machine gives me the freedom to create things tailored exactly to my vision. When presented with something that doesn't fit my needs, I know I can create something that does. My mom taught me to observe systems and seek answers to real-world problems. To understand people's needs and alleviate barriers, whether that's a comfortable mask, a translated ballot, or a life-saving medical device. I want to build a life where I can bridge the design thinking, prototyping, and building that I love with a real understanding of what the world needs. I want what I create to have a positive impact on the world; to be both a designer and a problem solver.

Essay 2, Final (Princeton!)

The man with the paint told me to look for "*catorce*," the one labeled "14."

Numbers have always comforted me. When I discovered times tables, I found power in concrete, quantitative mastery. When I first saw the variable *x* in place of a number, I recognized the potential of the unknown. I was twelve when the unknown truly revealed itself. I found the Seager equation, a series of variables that, when multiplied together, predict the number of extraterrestrial civilizations in our galaxy. It was beautiful. When I multiplied Seager's F_q by F_{hz}, I put reins on the universe and raced outward to find millions of extraterrestrial civilizations. I consumed, then questioned the equation. What if extraterrestrial beings float in space as machines, not bound to planets, not emitting biosignature gases? Do they want to be found? Anticipating that they don't, I proposed rights for extraterrestrial beings—rights to shelter, information, and amiability. With math as my justification and power, I found belonging in space.

But now I'm looking for 14. I scan the ground, kicking up dust, not believing my luck, thrilled. I find 14. I pick it up. I have an illogical fear that I'll drop it. It's heavy, perhaps more for its significance than its weight. I put it on the cinder block, then watch the man paint over the faded yellow with a bright, white 14. I'm on Isabela Island in the Galápagos, helping a National Park worker label a generation of tortoises. In 1835, when Nicholas Lawson pointed out that the tortoise shells have different forms on each Galápagos Island, he planted the seed in Charles Darwin's brain that grew into his evolutionary theory. When I held tortoise number 14, I held a million years of struggle and survival which sculpted that tortoise shell to its exact shape. "*Veintiséis*"—26—is next. I continue to search. If multiplying Seager variables shows me where I belong in space, then picking up a Galápagos tortoise shows me where I belong in time.

I find myself at a point of possibility in the expanse that equations and tortoises create, but the immensity makes it no easier to position my mind on Earth, where cultures diverge and clash. I grew up in a Harvard dorm where my parents were teachers and my mom was dean. I learned how to emulate college students. I learned to stand like they did, talk like they did, and think like they did. With the students as guides and with anthropologist parents, I came to my cultural understanding early. I learned about unconscious bias and systems of oppression before I learned the truth about Santa. Then, my family moved to a farm in Maryland. My mother cultivates the same iris flowers that my grandmother grew to put her through college.

In a small rural town, where North meets South and where traditional and progressive ideals sometimes clash, I find belonging by negotiating cultural understandings: I advocate for equity, climate action, and fair historical representation. If math runs in my blood, then I am morally compelled to use it to address the social injustices of the world and negotiate belonging for everyone.

Belonging is this responsibility to lead, but it's also a responsibility to listen, follow, and learn. My mom's research and my dad's ability to find cheap tickets led me to the Galápagos. Belonging is eating a bowl of fish stew and then, when my Ecuadorian hosts—fishermen and proud cooks—look away, eating my brothers' fish stew, because my cultural respect outweighs my long-standing vegetarianism (and my picky brothers won't eat their food). Belonging is the responsibility to learn all I can in order to be empathetic in my interactions and powerful in my change-making.

I pursue openings of unknowns where my brain belongs. I methodically and joyfully find my place in the expanse of time and space.

ADDENDUM ESSAY EXAMPLES

Essay 3, Final (University of Wisconsin, Madison!)

The variety of telephone poles on Earth is astounding. In Hungary, Romania, and Poland, oval holes perforate concrete poles; though, Romanian poles have white bases and Polish poles are skinny. In South America, step-like rungs climb ladder poles. In Ecuador, the rungs are spaced every two feet. In Brazil, every few meters. In France, angel-shaped metal structures suspend wires across the countryside. I study this as evidence of colonization. Senegalese pole tops are similar to those in France, its colonizer. French influence is all over West Africa. Would you be surprised to learn that Portuguese telephone poles are almost identical to Brazil's?

I am and always have been weirdly observant. When I was a kid, I moved slowly. I would stop on the way to school to observe every pebble and mark on the sidewalk. If my parents weren't dragging me along, I would have been late every day. Now, I travel farther and deeper into the world. There is no better feeling than connecting my studied knowledge to the places I visit.

In preparation for a trip to Italy, I studied. Because I am interested in history, I knew to focus on how people memorialize tragedy. In Rome, golden bricks announce houses where Holocaust victims lived. This past summer, as we walked the streets, I searched obsessively for the golden bricks. When we passed kosher restaurants, I suspected we were getting close. I found the first brick, then more. I collected the tragedies of history and now feel closer to my ancestors and the pain that has shaped my culture.

My desire to understand the history that makes a place combined with my ability to acutely observe has led to my interest in maps and geography. During quarantine, when I couldn't get out and see the world, I became obsessed with a game called *Geoguessr*. *Geoguessr* uses Google Street View to drop a player into a random location (a rural road, a neighborhood, a city corner). Then, the player uses clues in the digital images to guess their place. I connect the images I see with maps, melding cultural markers (clothes and people), environmental signatures (dirt color and landforms), and historical artifacts (buildings and architecture) to identify precise points. I know that in the states surrounding Ohio, cars have back license plates and no fronts. The dirt is whiter in western Botswana on the A2 highway than in eastern Botswana on the A1. I am freakishly good at this game, among the quantifiable best.

My other superpower is empathy, though it felt like a curse, at first. When I was five, I went to a college basketball game for ten minutes. From the moment I entered, I had a bad feeling. Buzzers, horns, and sirens blared. Though I knew the noises were part of the game, my brain went into overdrive. I had to get out ASAP. It wasn't just loud noises, though. Crowded parties, scratchy clothes, and emotional movies all sent me into crisis. Ends up, I am sensitive. Though some may view this as weakness, I now recognize it as strength. When I watch movies, I cannot handle the emotions of the characters. I find myself feeling their feelings and being sensitive to what happens to them, as if it were happening to me. Later in life, I learned that this is empathy. The depth of my empathy distinguishes me from others. I create comfort for people because their comfort is my own.

My ability to hyper fixate on how things affect people, my encyclopedic knowledge of geography and history, and some serious math skills have led to my college interest in Geography, GIS, and Cartography. I want to use statistics to create stories through maps. I want to harness my knowledge to make the world better.

Essay 4, First Rough Draft

In reflecting on my first three years of high school in order to write this essay, I realized something. It felt like there was a fairly even balance of happy and sad in everything that had happened so far, and as I was thinking about this, I realized that our whole lives are a lot like that too—walking a fine line between the good and bad, and always trying to make the good outweigh the bad. Maybe it's having a bad and stressful day, and then unexpectedly getting acai with friends over lunch, or it's losing an old friend, but reconnecting with those you'd grown apart from in order to grieve. Or it's starting off 2020 spending every day with your best friends and thinking it'll be the best year ever, and then suddenly not being able to see them for nearly four months. It's going in for help after school every day to make sure you really understand the physics unit you're struggling with, balanced with the joy when you get your report card with an A next to physics. It's having a swim season with a dream team of my friends, then not having a pool and practicing before school every day for months. And sometimes, we have periods where one greatly outweighs the other—like having a school dance one day, and going on a road trip to Ikea the next. Or when we have weeks with big tests and projects in every class throughout the week. The good must come with the bad, and vice versa. With everything that happens to us in our lives, more often than not, we try as hard as we can to highlight the moments that make us the happiest, and try to push away the sad moments. But, everything that happens makes us who we are. We exist in the space between happy and sad, good and bad, ecstasy and despair. While we cling to the best parts of our lives, we are also acknowledging the sad moments that have made them just that much sweeter. This is really a lot less black and white than this, I think that it's a pattern most of us can find some way in our lives.

Essay 4, Final (Vanderbilt!)

On a freezing midwestern day, my friends and I put on our warmest coats and walked quickly out of school, exchanging stories from our mundane days, making the most of our short lunch period. Our fingers froze in the winter wind outside the small yellow food truck as we received cold açaí bowls into our bare hands, the bright fruits and dark purple shocking against the pale white sidewalk and snow. Those fifty minutes transformed the mundane into meaningful.

Weeks later, I was assigned my third major physics project of the year: an elastic-powered vehicle. My best friend and I worked for hours every weekend for months. Halfway through, we realized we needed to start over. Stressed, we drove to Walmart to buy new supplies and, on impulse, purchased pink rhinestones. We spent the next weekend building our new car, and as a finishing touch, we covered the wheels with glittery rhinestones. The weeks of worry were worth the satisfaction of watching our shiny pink vehicle easily cross the target distance, earning an A on our project.

These small moments of joy are immensely valuable, but they are not perfect tools for a content life. Just over a year before, a friend of mine committed suicide. The news didn't hit me until hours after. The days between his death and funeral are a blur. I knew there could be no fix—I was completely out of control. I remember talking to friends I hadn't spoken to in years to reminisce through our grief. Rekindling old friendships and helping each other cope provided comfort and familiarity in a situation that sorely lacked both.

It is not too difficult to find equilibrium in a life when even my greatest tragedies can be helped by a supportive network; but I've long had a sense that other lives have complexities I cannot fix, no matter how badly I want to. Getting involved in activism has provided me with a grander active engagement with the world, and the ability to help in situations I previously believed were out of my control.

During my freshman spring, I organized protests and school walkouts for gun control. I worked with a group of upperclassmen I'd never met, but we found quick comfort in our collective passion. I became a founding member of an activist network composed of community members, high school students, and college students. We have grown exponentially from our original fifteen as we continue to organize teach-ins, protests, and more. As the youngest member of this group, I feel the responsibility to continue our momentum.

As a sophomore, I started a chapter of Junior State of America. I persevered, encouraging students to engage with pressing societal and political issues, though many claimed they were "not into politics." This spring, when renewed global support of the Black Lives Matter movement proved not even a pandemic could stop centuries of racism and injustice, I watched as many of the students, who were previously uninterested in politics, educated themselves. They taught me that progress often takes time. I now recognize how much work must be done to achieve equality, and how I can use my privilege to help those who lack it.

I hope to continue this work by becoming a human rights attorney. The more I become aware of the world's problems and injustices, the more I want to fix them. These are massive systemic issues that cannot be easily fixed, but I want to take my next step in making change with a double major in psychology and public policy—one to learn about introspective changes we can make as individuals, and the other to learn what we can do for our society. Our world is failing myriads of its people, but there has to be a way to fix our systems so that açaí bowls, pink rhinestones, and old friends can be enough for all.

Essay 5, First Rough Draft

When I was younger, I felt really connected to nature and its life force. My mom and I would go walking and camping in the woods with our two dogs, Cocoa and Journey. I would climb big rocks and try to find a leaf as big as my head and let Daddy Long Legs (Cellar Spiders) climb all over me. While we walked, I could hear the birds singing, the crickets chirping and the leaves and twigs crunching under our feet. I liked to think about how even in the calm, peaceful environment, there was a bustling life force all around us. Birds were finding food for their babies, ants were looking for crumbs and squirrels were hiding food for the winter. I think about this a lot, even when I'm not surrounded by nature.

I see a similar energy in cities and communities. I love seeing new people and knowing they have completely different lives and experiences, but just for a second, we're in the same place at the same time and have a small, fleeting connection. Whether we were in the same coffee shop or watching the same sunset, we connected for just a moment. Even if we didn't know it. We are all individuals with different lives but also have a sense of community. This connection is part of the reason I want to go into journalism. I love connecting with people and learning more about them. If I could continue to do that while writing impactful, meaningful articles, I would be unexplainably grateful.

I believe, since we grow up in social environments, we, as people, develop a need for purpose, which usually has some aspect of giving back. Firefighters and police work to keep us safe. The government works to protect us and our rights. As a journalist, I hope to innovate positive change, reshape conversations, expose truth, amplify underrepresented voices and cultivate diversity.

As I pursue a career in journalism, I will bring the lessons I've learned from walking in the woods with my family—the importance of observation, connection, and empathy. Different aspects of life mirror itself, like the woods and a city. My goal is to write articles that not only informs but also inspires, ignites conversations, and encourages readers to look beyond themselves. To truly connect we must understand each other and learn to look at the world from a new perspective.

Essay 5, Final (American!)

When I was younger, I would go walking in the woods with my dogs. I would climb rocks and try to find a leaf as big as my head. I'd let daddy long legs climb all over me. While the birds sang, the crickets chirped, and twigs crunched, I liked to think about how even in the calm, peaceful environment, birds were finding food for their babies, ants were looking for crumbs, and squirrels were hiding food for the winter. I think about these biological connections a lot, even when I'm not surrounded by nature.

As an adopted Guatemalan American girl with two moms and a step-mom, biological connections play a complicated role in my life. My moms found me when I was an infant, but I didn't come home until I was one. I was lost in a raid on the orphanage, and then found. I was interested in finding my birth mom when I was younger. We thought we found her on Facebook and we contacted her, but if it was her, she either didn't answer or didn't want to be contacted. I don't remember. I am connected with Guatemala, though. I have a G-fam. There are ten of us, from that orphanage that was raided in 2007. We have a group chat, and we're friends on social media. We meet in person every couple of years. Outside of my G-fam, I also have many caring, generous, and thoughtful friends. None of these connections are biological, but they are profound.

I don't just love nature, I love cities, too. I see a similar connected energy in urban communities. I love seeing strangers and knowing they have completely different lives and experiences; but just for a second, we're in the same place at the same time, maybe in a coffee shop breathing in the coffee smell together, or collectively experiencing the glow of a sunset. And we have a small, fleeting connection.

I understand this emotional connection even without physical closeness. There's a boy in Guatemala who had a crib next to mine. We were close. We are close. I don't know him. I don't remember this time in my life. My mom told me about it. But it's important.

I don't like being vulnerable or talking about my feelings. I don't always trust people. I'm working on this. When you're a Guatemalan pan-sexual kid with a variety of adoptive mothers, one receives tricky feedback from the world, from time to time. This can make trust hard.

In nature, as a whole, things may look perfect. Branches will sway in the wind, the sun will shine through the leaves, but when you look closer, things are not as perfect as they may seem. Sometimes my life may look more put together than it is, but that's okay. I know I can figure out how to get where I want to be. I like solving problems. I believe that all the problems we have in the world now ultimately have a solution. But we need to work together, understand each other, and listen to each other in order to find those solutions.

As a journalist, I hope to innovate positive change, reshape conversations, expose truth, amplify underrepresented voices, and cultivate diversity.

I will bring the lessons I've learned from walking in the woods with my family: the importance of observation, connection, and empathy. My goal is to write articles that not only inform but also inspire, ignite conversations, and encourage readers to look beyond themselves. To truly connect, regardless of physical and emotional proximity, we must understand each other and learn to look at the world from a new perspective.

Essay 6, First Rough Draft

I'm very interested in what draws human attention, whether its sounds or colors, maybe when your driving on a highway and see a brightly colored fast food sign out of the corner of your eye and suddenly realize how hungry you are, or when you hear a certain jingle while scrolling on your phone and you look up at your tv and see the product that you forgot that you needed. When I try to sleep, in a dark and quiet room, my attention is always being dragged to any small thing that I can see or hear. A creak on the floor, or guessing whose footsteps were coming up the stairs or maybe the fly that I can hear buzzing around my room makes it hard for me to fall asleep. Sleep has always been an issue for me throughout my life for as long as I can remember. I would spend many nights looking up at my wall, feeling too tired to stand up, but too awake to close my eyes and I would just think about everything that happened to me that day or maybe everything I thought was going to happen to me the next day. It seemed like at night I had so many things to think about and my mind would just wander on to any and every topic imaginable, from penguins to my next math class to the time I got a scar on my arm from jumping over a fence playing tag with my friends. Before I knew it, it would be 3am and somehow it would feel like 1 minute had passed and 5 hours had passed at the same time. When i was a kid, i hated having to go to sleep and never wanted to nap, but now i look forward to going to bed and recovering from my day and feel lucky whenever i can take a nap. The best sleep i think ive ever gotten was when I got uprgraded on a flight from the Philippines to JFK, a 16 hour flight, and the best part was that my whole family got upgraded alongside me. As i sat down in my huge seat i process the smell of fresh orange juice as im handed a warm towel, i feel my back submerge into the soft cushion of the seat and am in shock as i look around and see the huge movie like tv screen in my own seat that i cant even see well unless I put on my glasses, the huge amount of leg room where even when i extended my legs as far as they could go i still had so much space left, then out of the corner of my eye i noticed a remote built intothe seat, glowing with a soft blue light, as i pressed each of the buttons, my seat started to move; back, forward, 90 degrees, 180 degrees, and everything in between, i look to my right and see my mom and sister who also mustve just noticed the remote as their seat was moving up and down. To my left i see my dad scrolling and looking at all the movies he wants to watch on the huge personal TV. My family being there with me made me feel so at home even though i was across the globe and 30 thousand feet in the sky. I made the chair turn into a reclined position, then into a full flat bed. I grab the soft blanket and pillow that were provided to me as i boarded the flight and fell asleep it what felt like less then a minute, i remember sleeping for almost 10 hours, which is probably double the amount ive ever got on the plane before, and waking up thinking that was the best sleep i had ever had. I wake up to the scent of warm bread as we are being served breakfast, i take my bread and get served a soft and fluffy french toast with fresh fruit as well. I couldnt believe i was in a plane as just 2 weeks before on my flight to the philippines my seat wouldnt recline and i felt like i had no space. Every time i go to the philippines i dread the long flight, but when i get there i realize how every second of the flight was worth it. Im greeted by my older and younger cousins, my titos and titas, and feel so happy, while also missing my lolo and lola. When i sit down and eat and get served rice and hot dogs, and as i look up i always feel a resemblance to my other side of the family, where everything felt so different, yet so similar at the same time. Saying grace before eating in the philippines reminds me of reading from the torah on passover in my home town, and my big filipino family sitting and the round table reminds me of my big jewish family eating at the huge table in my Uncle and aunts house, and the rice and hotdogs reminds me of the brisket and matzoh.

Being half Ahkenazi jewish and half Filipino is something that has affected my life greatly and taught me many lessons. The most being the importance of family, family will always be there for you and will always be apart of you, no matter if you are across the globe or in the same town, in the Philippines or in highland park New jersey, eating hotdogs and rice or brisket and matzoh. Ive never met somebody with the same ethnic background as me, and I feel nobody ive met can really relate to the expirience that i have, having two families with completely different cultures and religions, living on opposite sides of the globe, yet being taught the same important lessons by both sides.

Essay 6, Final (Fordham!)

I have always had a complicated relationship with sleep. Throughout my life, there were countless nights when I lay awake at 3 a.m., hearing every creak, every footstep, every faint fly-buzzing. My thoughts would flow freely. I could think unrestrictedly. It was my time, after one day ended, and before another began, to drift far from reality. I thought about what I could and would do the next day as if I were living twelve hours ahead of time. On these nights, I would imagine that the Filipino in me (my mother is from the Philippines), was living my Filipino life. After all, 3 a.m. here is 3 p.m. there, so it made perfect sense that I couldn't sleep.

I imagined my Filipino family, sitting at the huge, round table in my *lolo*'s house in Tahanan village, eating rice and adobo. I imagined going to the mall in Manila to buy cheesy fries from Potato Corner. I imagined being surrounded by the people who define me, despite my home being across the world. Growing up in the United States, I kept my Filipino side close at night, while living my waking hours with my Ashkenazi Jewish family, which more conveniently exists in Eastern Standard Time. My four cousins are older than me and well known in my town. "Weinberg" announces my relationships, and I am proud of them. On Jewish holidays, we gather at my aunt and late uncle's house, at a huge rectangular dinner table loaded with brisket and matzah. The gatherings are always lively with old-friend drama and political debate.

The two sides of me resemble each other, despite the polarized differences, the churches and synagogues, the spicy and the unleavened. My different heritages teach me the same thing. The community and people I surround myself with are vital to my life and character. Family is important. Connection is love.

As I entered high school, I knew that my Filipino side couldn't continue to roam around all night long in my imagination. I needed sleep. I devised a plan. I forced myself to be home before

11 p.m. I showered, brushed my teeth, and went to bed. This took determination and consistency, but I did it. The summer presented new challenges. In the morning, I would sleep in, making it hard to sleep at night. I enacted part B of my plan. As the captain of my soccer team, I scheduled all summer practices to begin at 7:30 a.m. Forty teammates relied on me to run practices at the crack of dawn; I couldn't sleep in and let them down. This new sleep routine, I justified, was good for them, too.

But none of these self-help routines would have been possible had I not figured out a way to seal the time gap between the two sides of the world and the two sides of myself. On a recent flight back from the Philippines, my family was upgraded to business class. The stewards greeted us with warm towels and freshly squeezed orange juice. I looked to my right. My mom and sister excitedly tried to press "Play," at the exact same moment, on their seats' TV screens to sync their experiences. To my left, my dad giddily scrolled through countless entertainment options. I felt unparalleled joy when I realized my seat turned into a full lay-flat bed. I put on my eye mask, turned my TV off, and laid my seat back. On that seventeen-hour flight, thirty thousand feet in the air, traveling between my two amazing yet distant worlds with my closest people, I had the best sleep of my entire life. It was the most at home I've ever felt.

At that moment, I realized that, for me, sleep isn't just rest; it's what connects me to my roots, my family, and my identity. It lets me feel truly at home no matter where I am.

ACKNOWLEDGMENTS

It is impossible to identify all the moments that cause us to wonder about this world and our place within it, the processes at the heart of this book. But I am certain of a few. Our open-eyed identity formation must start when we're little, when the people around us teach us how to sense our surroundings in new ways. When my dad showed me that constellations might be upside-down for me and right-side up for others, and when my mom dragged the algae from the lake onto her belly to inspect it rather than avoiding the green slime like the other mothers, I learned to see. Thank you!

My brothers and sisters (the ones who have been with me forever and those who joined us later), my parental figures of all kinds (here and passed on), my nieces and nephews—each one so beautiful and unique: To share raviolis, beer, brisket, board games, trivia, puzzles, epic athletic feats, books, and brave writing is pure delight. Thank you!

I must thank my Illinois people for making my own college experience so amazing. I am forever grateful for the driving, striving, struggling, porch-sitting, future-pondering, traveling, justice-making, security-giving. Oh, you are foundational.

Thank you, to my Teach for America friends, for having the faith and courage to shift systems.

And thank you to my friends at the Mosaic Project and Global Routes. You have opened so many eyes, minds, and hearts, including mine.

To my anthropology cohort and professors at the University of Michigan, who helped me understand power and all the forces that obstruct and illuminate, thank you.

So much gratitude to my colleagues and friends in the Expository Writing Department at Harvard and the Sweetland Writing Center at Michigan who taught me the magical formulas for impactful writing and thinking. You have launched a million vectors of brilliance and world-betterment through your work.

Thank you to my students at Harvard and Michigan who gnashed their teeth with me as we identified the holes in thought through which compassion might shine. Thank you to the students before them—at Northwest High School in Halifax County, in Puerto Villamil on Isabela Island, and at Holly Park in Seattle. With your joy, ingenuity, and resilience, you have taught me the depth of character and strength.

I am so grateful for my colleagues at Cabot House and in the administration of Harvard, who helped me figure out how to structure community and make space for audacious pursuits. You are nurturing, fair, kind, and visionary.

Thank you to my college applicants—the students and their families who sat with me in the barn, in the library (thank you, librarians! All librarians!), at our tables, on FaceTime, across email. I am deeply honored that you have trusted me with your amazing stories. May you thrive!

Thank you to all the editors of this book, of past and future books, of student essays, of hard texts, of life thoughts. Clarity, concision, attention, brave criticism, and loving support set new ideas free.

Of course, this book would not be possible without Jake Bonar of Prometheus Books and Jill Marsal of Marsal Lyon Literary Agency. Jake, your confidence in this project and your warmth in all of our interactions have been validating, generous, and generative. You have encouraged and then channeled my flightier notions,

ACKNOWLEDGMENTS

giving me the space to think freely and the confidence to rein it in. Jill, you are fast, certain, and so smart. For all I know and write about the desperate and emotional difficulties of writing, the two of you, somehow, have made this book feel easy. I'm a bit baffled, really. Such solidity in such a vulnerable process has made all the difference. You are true gems.

And thank you to my dear friends from Lake of the Woods, Champaign/Urbana, Chicago, Halifax County, Seattle, Isabela, Santa Cruz, Oakland, Ann Arbor, Bahia, Cambridge, and Middletown—parents and caregivers of all kinds. I am a skittish friend, jumping from place to place, often having the urge to leave before I mess things up. You have held on through so many transitions, through all the joy, all the worry, all the adoration and despair, all the frustration and success, always with deep analysis, support, laughter, and love. To be a woman in this world, working all the puzzles, setting boundaries, and kicking those boundaries over, I would be lost without your support. I have somehow gathered the best people in the universe to take me through, to work this world and these lives to their maximum earth-shattering beauty. I hope that, through this book, your strength, wisdom, and love may reverberate across all the caregivers' lives as it has across my life.

Rio, Sol, Rafa, and Carmelo. My dear babies. It is sometimes hard to know where we begin and end; our tangled little mat of love is so strong, so funny, so wise, and weird that I only know my existence through its hold. You are everything.

Michael, who has the strength and absolute sweetness to hang in with me through it all (this old farm, our babies, our own audacious pursuits), I have insisted on ways of living that require so much energy. You promised me that you would embrace my unconventional ways. I see how fully you have kept this promise, burning, burning, burning with me, all the way to the end. No regrets. I love you.

www.ingramcontent.com/pod-product-compliance
Lightning Source LLC
LaVergne TN
LVHW041630060526
838200LV00040B/1526